THE SWISS ECONOMY
IN A NUTSHELL

CYRIL JOST
VINCENT KUCHOLL
MIX & REMIX

Bergli

Acknowledgements by the authors

We express our gratitude to Aymo Brunetti, Cécile Collet, Olivier Engler, Hervé Froidevaux, Rinny Gremaud, Alexander Jost, Brigitte Kauffmann, Philippe Kenel, Luca Perazzi, Nicolas Peter, Hervé Ramoni, Joëlle Simond, Yves Steiner et Matthias Urban for their careful reading of this work.

Many thanks also to Michael Hermann, of the 'sotomo' Research Institute of Zurich University (pp. 24–25), and to the *Handelszeitung* and its publisher Axel Springer Schweiz for permission to use their data (p. 38).

Translator's acknowledgements

Many thanks to Roderick Abbott for his invaluable advice on GATT and WTO.

Originally published in French by LEP Loisirs et Pédagogie SA, Lausanne, copyright 2007, revised edition copyright 2021
French edition ISBN 978-2-606-01691-3
LEP Series Manager: Vincent Kucholl
Original French edition cover: Moser Design SA, Lausanne
Original French design and production: NK Éditions,
Le Mont-sur-Lausanne

Contents

Challenges for the Swiss economy

Introduction

The economy is everywhere. It affects our daily life from its simplest form – the choice of what to buy or how to pay a bill – to its most complex – central bank policy or the signature of a free trade agreement.

Economics is not reserved for specialists. You don't need to be a mechanic to understand what makes a car run, and you don't need a prestigious degree to understand the general functioning of the Swiss economy.

Starting with a few basic notions and using examples specific to Switzerland, this book offers a wide perspective of economics and the main mechanisms and issues involved.

Understanding the terminology of economics is helped by the book's clear and simple explanations, as well as by the glossary and index.

We are all economic actors: analysing and understanding the 'rules of the game' will enable us to play our part in society.

What is the economy?

Economics deals with the way in which society uses limited resources to meet everyone's needs.

Various disciplines

Microeconomics
The study of individual economic behaviour.

For example: how does a smoker react if the price of cigarettes rises?

Macroeconomics
The study of economic phenomena as they affect society.

For example: what can the government do to reduce unemployment?

Political economy
The combination of micro- and macroeconomics to determine policy. The emphasis may be on the means of **acquisition of wealth** or, on the contrary, its **distribution**.

Some great thinkers

- Adam Smith (1723–1790) and David Ricardo (1772–1823) founded the doctrine of **classic liberalism**.
- Karl Marx (1818–1883) based his criticism of capitalism on the concept of class struggle. He was one of the founders of **communism**.

- John Maynard Keynes (1883–1946) emphasised the importance of **State** intervention in the economy as a means to ensure full employment.
- Friedrich von Hayek (1899–1992) and Milton Friedman (1912–2006) founded **neo-liberalism**, postulating minimal State intervention in the economy.

The liberal market economy

- The theory of the *homo economicus* – one of the founding principles of liberalism – is based on the assumption that every human being acts **rationally,** in relation to what he/she finds **useful.**

- As a result of the **division of labour,** each of us specialises in the sector in which his/her productivity is highest. This is the basis of **capitalism,** which stimulates private enterprise and the search for profit.

- Economic liberalism is founded on a simple proposition: the more that humans are free to **produce** and **trade** in a **market,** the more wealth they will create.

  Switzerland has a liberal economic structure. As a result of the country's geographical situation and the absence of natural resources, it has always depended strongly on external trade.

The word 'liberal' does not have the same meaning for everyone. In French, it is often used in the economic sense to describe an anti-interventionist policy favourable to the free market; this is supported mainly by political parties on the right. In English, the same word describes movements opposed to conservatism, and is mainly supported by parties on the left.

The theory of comparative advantage developed by David Ricardo in 1817

Phase 1: there is no trade between countries

A Portuguese producer can make one unit of cloth or three barrels of wine per day.

An English producer can make three units of cloth or one barrel of wine per day.

Phase 2: each country specialises

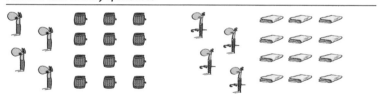

The Portuguese produce only wine.

The English only produce cloth.

Phase 3:

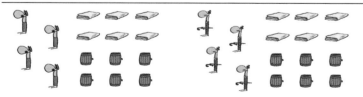

By specialising and trading, each country obtains more wine and more cloth than if they were producing only for themselves. Everyone gains.

Economic flows

The four main participants in the economy are households, companies, the State and banks. 'Economic flows' are exchanges of money, goods or services between them.

1 | Workers provide the **labour** that allows companies to create added value.
┄┄⟩ *The three sectors (p. 12)*
┄┄⟩ *Trade unions (p. 48)*

2 | **Companies** pay workers salaries in exchange for their work.
┄┄⟩ *Legal structures (p. 36)*
┄┄⟩ *Companies large and small (p. 38)*
┄┄⟩ *Entrepreneurs (p. 40)*
┄┄⟩ *Company accounting (p. 42)*

3 | With the money earned, workers can **buy** the goods and services they need.
┄┄⟩ *Supply and demand (p. 52)*
┄┄⟩ *Competition (p. 54)*
┄┄⟩ *Prices (p. 56)*
┄┄⟩ *Inflation (p. 58)*
┄┄⟩ *Currency (p. 62)*

4 | Workers must pay **taxes** to the State; companies too.
┄┄⟩ *Taxation (p. 28)*

5 | The **State** makes investments that are of benefit to the whole population (by building roads, for example).
⤑ *Economic policy (p. 22)*
⤑ *Public finance (p. 26)*
⤑ *Public companies (p. 46)*

6 | Employees can deposit part of their earnings with a **bank**. Companies can borrow money to make new investments and expand their activities.
⤑ *The Swiss National Bank (p. 64)*
⤑ *Banks (p. 66)*

7 | Employees can also **invest** part of their earnings.
⤑ *Stock markets (p. 70)*
⤑ *Financial products (P. 72)*

8 | Rises in the income of employees lead to higher consumption of goods and services and contribute to economic **growth** in general.
⤑ *GDP (p. 16)*

9 | A national economy does not operate in a closed circuit; it is subject to **international competition**.
⤑ *Globalisation of the economy (p. 80)*
⤑ *The WTO (p. 82)*
⤑ *Switzerland and Europe (p. 84)*
⤑ *The open economy (p. 92)*

10 | Economic growth does not benefit everyone in the same way. It can have negative effects.
⤑ *Economic cycles (p. 18)*
⤑ *Unemployment (p. 32)*
⤑ *The 2007–2008 financial crisis (p. 74)*
⤑ *Disparities (p. 94)*
⤑ *The economy and the environment (p. 96)*

The national economy

The three sectors

The economy comprises three sectors: primary, secondary and tertiary.

The primary sector

(2.5% of the active population of Switzerland in 2020)

In Switzerland, this sector comprises essentially **agriculture**, which has declined substantially during the last decades. With the reduction of federal subsidies, many farms can no longer survive.

The secondary sector

(20.9% of the active population of Switzerland in 2020)

Swiss **industry** employs today less manpower than in the recent past, especially in textiles and mechanical engineering. Some branches require a high degree of precision and quality; these, such as watch-making and pharmaceutical production, have grown.

The tertiary sector

(76.6% of the active population of Switzerland in 2020)

The tertiary sector is dominated by services: trade, insurance, banking, tourism, health, education, public administration, etc.

In the mid-1960s, the Paillard company was known throughout the world for its *Hermès* typewriters and its *Bolex* cameras. It had some 6000 employees at factories in Yverdon and Sainte-Croix. Ten years later, the company was closed down – a symbol of industrial decline in Switzerland. The population of Sainte-Croix went from 6900 in 1960 to 4850 today.

Changes in employment by sector in Switzerland

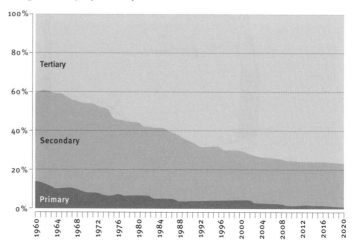

The explosion of the tertiary sector

- In developed countries, the tertiary sector has seen major growth in the 20th century. It marks the shift to the **post-industrial society**.

- **Globalisation** (····⟩ p. 80) has accelerated this process. Countries with a very high educational level (like Switzerland) have been able to concentrate on services with high added value, based on **knowledge and information**. Agricultural and industrial production has shifted to less developed countries.

- The development in rich countries of **leisure** activities (tourism, cinemas, theme parks, etc.) has also contributed to the growth of the tertiary sector.

- An ageing population also creates demand for new services, particularly in health care.

HIGH TECH ↓ **ADDED VALUE** ↙

Saving industry?

- Faced with the decline of the secondary sector, some countries have chosen **interventionist policies** (····⟩ p. 22).

  In France, a number of politicians consider that the State should implement an 'industrial policy' to counteract industrial decline.

- In Switzerland, most political actors oppose measures that would give favourable treatment to the industrial sector in particular.

Following the 2007–2008 financial crisis, the American and Canadian governments put in place a rescue plan for the North-American automobile industry. With 85 billion dollars of financial support, they prevented the almost certain bankruptcy of the three giants of the industry: General Motors, Ford and Chrysler.

The three sectors

Most Swiss companies are in the secondary and tertiary sectors. Here are a few examples.

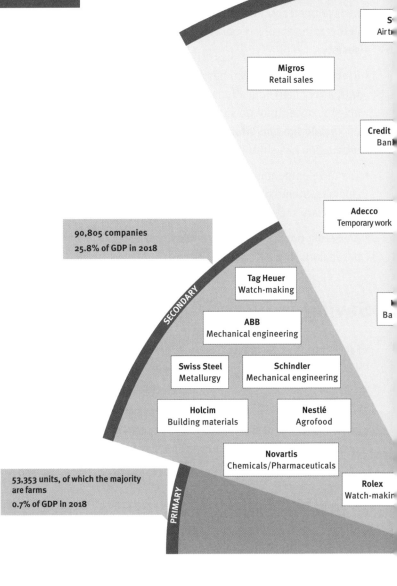

S...
Air t...

Migros
Retail sales

Credit
Ban...

Adecco
Temporary work

90,805 companies
25.8% of GDP in 2018

SECONDARY

Tag Heuer
Watch-making

ABB
Mechanical engineering

...
Ba...

Swiss Steel
Metallurgy

Schindler
Mechanical engineering

Holcim
Building materials

Nestlé
Agrofood

Novartis
Chemicals/Pharmaceuticals

53,353 units, of which the majority are farms
0.7% of GDP in 2018

PRIMARY

Rolex
Watch-makin...

EVOLUTION

NATURE　　FACTORY　　OFFICE　　RETURN TO NATURE

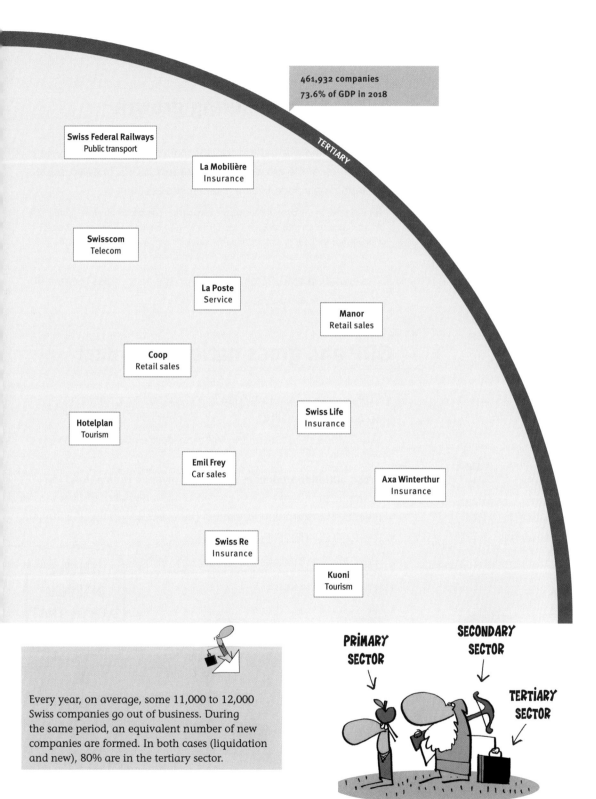

461,932 companies
73.6% of GDP in 2018

TERTIARY

Swiss Federal Railways
Public transport

La Mobilière
Insurance

Swisscom
Telecom

La Poste
Service

Manor
Retail sales

Coop
Retail sales

Swiss Life
Insurance

Hotelplan
Tourism

Emil Frey
Car sales

Axa Winterthur
Insurance

Swiss Re
Insurance

Kuoni
Tourism

PRIMARY SECTOR

SECONDARY SECTOR

TERTIARY SECTOR

Every year, on average, some 11,000 to 12,000 Swiss companies go out of business. During the same period, an equivalent number of new companies are formed. In both cases (liquidation and new), 80% are in the tertiary sector.

The gross domestic product is the total value of goods and services produced in a defined area in a year.

A tool for measuring growth

- In Switzerland, the federal statistical office produces every year a calculation of the **gross domestic product** (GDP). To avoid double-counting, only added value is taken into account.

  For example, in the case of cheese, the calculation comprises the price of milk (the value added by the farmer), the cost of production (value added by the cheese-maker) and the cost of distribution (the value added by the distributor). The combined added value gives the final price of cheese.

- The evolution of GDP from one year to the next shows the rate of growth of the economy.

GDP and gross national product

GDP is the result of the activity of millions of human beings. In 2018, Swiss GDP (population 8 million and 20th economy in the world) was 690 billion francs.

- **GDP** comprises all production in a given territory, taking no account of nationality.

  Swiss GDP is the wealth generated by all persons and companies established in Switzerland.

- **Gross national product** also includes revenue from abroad (for example, profits of a Swiss company operating abroad), less revenue transferred to foreigners (for example, profits of a foreign company operating in Switzerland).

  The Swiss gross national product comprises the wealth generated by Swiss persons and companies operating in Switzerland and abroad.

An international basis for comparison

GDP allows comparative measurement of different economies

GDP of the main world economies in 2018

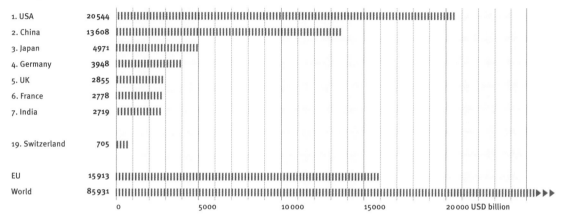

1. USA	20 544
2. China	13 608
3. Japan	4971
4. Germany	3948
5. UK	2855
6. France	2778
7. India	2719
19. Switzerland	705
EU	15 913
World	85 931

0   5000   10 000   15 000   20 000 USD billion

GDP per capita in 2016

Luxembourg	116 597
Switzerland	82 829
Norway	81 735
Ireland	78 583
Iceland	73 368
Qatar	68 794
Singapore	64 582
USA	62 887

0   20 000   40 000   60 000   80 000   100 000 USD

The limits of GDP

- GDP gives no indication of the **distribution of wealth** in an economy or of the 'underground' economy (e.g. black market).

- Some countries use **unreliable statistics** in determining their GDP – in these cases, comparison can only be approximate.

- Inter-country comparisons require conversion into US dollars. But **exchange rates** fluctuate, adding another level of approximation.

Annual GDP growth

	Switzerland	China
2007	4.1%	14.2%
2008	2.2%	9.7%
2009	−2.2%	9.4%
2010	3.0%	10.6%
2011	1.7%	9.5%
2012	1.0%	7.9%
2013	1.9%	7.8%
2014	2.4%	7.3%
2015	1.3%	6.9%
2016	1.7%	6.7%
2017	1.8%	6.8%
2018	2.8%	6.6%

Economic cycles

By observing the GDP of a country over several years, it is possible to identify periods of expansion (when production increases) and recession (when production stagnates or falls). These periods, that can be more or less regular, are known as economic cycles.

The first references to economic cycles can be found in the Bible: the seven 'fat' years of great abundance that follow on seven 'lean' years of famine.

The four phases of the cycle

Expansion
The economy is prospering, GDP is increasing year on year. This period, known as '**boom**', is characterised by increasing investment, consumption, income and prices. Unemployment goes down.

Crisis
Growth slows and stops (**stagnation**). Crisis marks the point at which the growth curve begins to turn downwards. In day-to-day language, the term crisis is used to denote a recession.

Recession
During this period the economy **slumps** – characterised by near-zero growth or even a **fall in production** (some economists describe it as 'negative growth'). The level of investment and income goes down and unemployment increases. If a recession goes on over a long period, it is called a **depression**.

Pickup
This is the point at which the economy starts growing again and begins a new expansionary period.

Some major crises

- The **crash of 1929** was a crisis at the New York Stock Exchange that marked the beginning of the Great Depression of the 1930s.

- The **oil shock** of 1973 put an end to the three decades of prosperity that followed World War II. It caused massive inflation and a world-wide recession.

- The **internet bubble** that burst in 2000 was the consequence of frantic speculation in the shares of start-up companies in areas of new technology.

- The US **subprime** mortgage crisis led to the world financial crisis of 2007–2008 (····} p. 74).

- The **coronavirus pandemic** provoked a **world economic crisis in 2020**.

State intervention

- The State may attempt to **control cycles** through massive expenditure programmes during a recession, in order to revive growth (····} p. 22).

  Following the 1929 crisis, US President Franklin D. Roosevelt launched a vast programme of investment, known as the New Deal. In 2020, the USA, the European Union and other countries put stimulative measures in place to get out of the crisis.

- The State may use **monetary policy** (····} p. 65) to influence growth and inflation.

In the days following the Wall Street crash of 1929, there were press reports in New York of suicides. Many investors could not bear having lost everything and threw themselves out of their office windows.

Economic cycles

In the short term, it is often difficult to determine the cyclic phase of the economy. With time, it is possible to distinguish clearly long periods of expansion and recession.

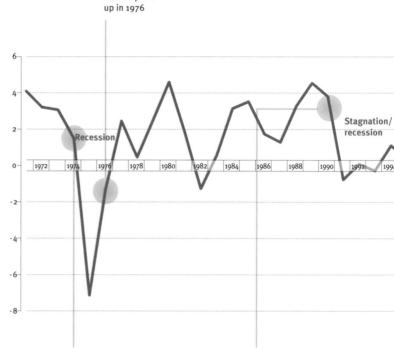

Annual GDP growth in Switzerland (%)

Growth picks up in 1976

Recession

Stagnation/recession

Switzerland, like most other countries in the world, was in a deep recession in the mid 1970s.

At the beginning of the 1990s, Switzerland suffered a real estate crisis, followed by a long period of marked stagnation. This slowing of the economy was due to globalisation, which forced much restructuring of the economy.

The Russian economist Nikolai Kondratiev worked out a theory of cycles showing that capitalist economies recover after a crisis. His theories led to his being deported to prison camp by Stalin, where he was shot in 1938.

I'M STAGNATING!

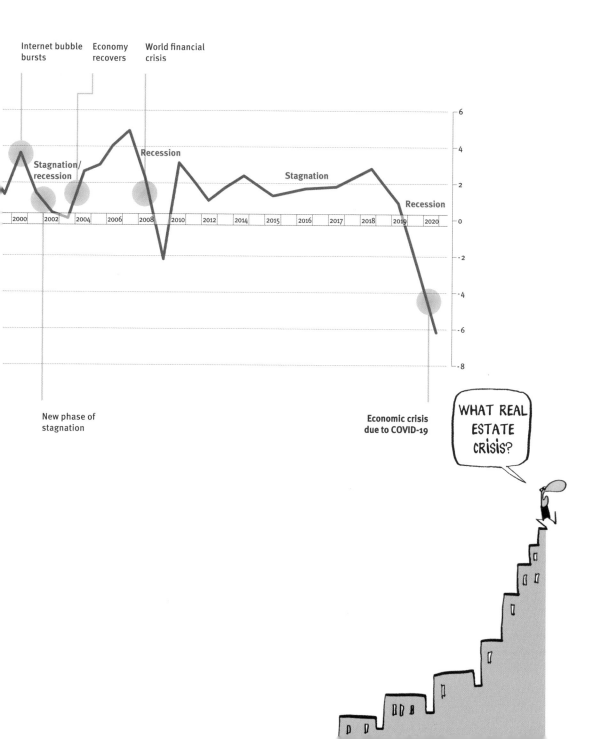

Economic policy

A State's economic policy may encourage growth and attempt to correct market imbalances. There are two main opposing theories: the Keynesian, that proposes State intervention in the economy; and the 'liberal', that allows the market to regulate itself.

Interventionism

- The State may intervene in the economy by playing an important **adjustment** role, according to the theory of the English economist **John Maynard Keynes** in the 1930s.

- Keynes showed that during a recession the State can increase its expenditure (at the price of going deeply into debt) in order to create **jobs** and revive the economy. This is called a **counter-cyclical** budget policy, because the State attempts to counteract the economic cycle (····> p. 18).

- The Keynesian theory was responsible for the economic policies of most Western countries from the time of World War II until the beginning of the 1980s.

- Interventionist policies are usually supported by parties of the **left**.

  Switzerland was never able to implement a true Keynesian policy, because the Confederation does not have complete control of all public expenditure. As a result of the country's federal structure, much expenditure is covered by cantonal and communal budgets.

Liberalism

On 10 April 1947, the future Nobel prize-winner Milton Friedman invited liberal thinkers from around the world to the shores of Lake Geneva, above Vevey (canton of Vaud) for the founding of the 'Mont-Pelerin Society'. It was within this network of intellectuals that neoliberalism was born, an economic policy adopted by many States today.

- A much more liberal theory, proposing minimal State intervention in the economy, was developed in the 1960s by the economist **Milton Friedman**.

- According to him, the State should limit its role to controlling inflation through **monetary policy** (····> p. 65).

- During the 1980s, this thinking greatly influenced the governments of Ronald Reagan in the USA and Margaret Thatcher in the UK.

- Liberal economic policies are usually supported by parties of the **right**.

Switzerland, a liberal economy

- Since the collapse of the communist bloc, most countries follow a **liberal** economic policy. This is characterised by the **withdrawal** of the State (privatisation) and **deregulation** of markets (liberalisation).

- Swiss economic policy is very liberal in certain areas, for example in **tax** policy (low by international comparison) or in the **labour market** (very flexible).

- In other areas, Swiss economic policy is less liberal; **agriculture**, for example, is highly subsidised by the State.

NOTHING GROWS WITHOUT IT!

External trade

Switzerland has defined the following priorities for its **foreign trade policy**:
- encouragement of foreign trade (┈┈┊> p. 92);
- increased competition on the internal market (┈┈┊> p. 93);
- aid to developing countries as future trading partners (┈┈┊> p. 87).

COMPETITION ON THE INTERNAL MARKET

In Switzerland, public expenditure (communal, cantonal and federal) represented 32% of GDP in 2018. In most European countries, this proportion is much higher; in France: 56%; and Denmark: 51%

Economic policy

Each political party has an economic policy that can be called liberal or interventionist.

This classification is based on studies by the sotomo Research Institute of Zurich University of the voting patterns on economic issues of Swiss federal parliamentarians.

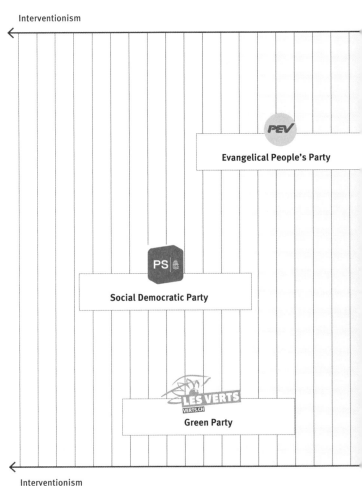

Interventionism

Evangelical People's Party

Social Democratic Party

Green Party

Interventionism

THE RICH MUST GIVE TO THE POOR!

SOLIDARITY

- The **extreme left** seeks **strong State intervention**, mainly for the redistribution of wealth to the poorer classes. It favours high taxation of the wealthy and of companies.

- The **left** seeks **moderate State intervention**, mainly to regulate markets and redistribute wealth. It favours moderate taxation, in order not to threaten growth.

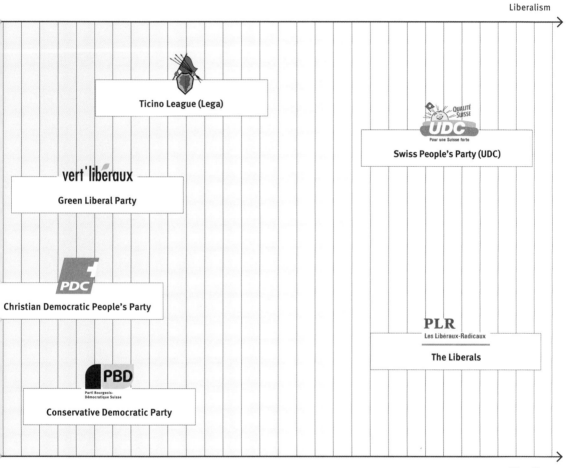

Liberalism

Ticino League (Lega)

Swiss People's Party (UDC)

vert'libéraux
Green Liberal Party

PDC
Christian Democratic People's Party

PLR
Les Libéraux-Radicaux
The Liberals

PBD
Parti Bourgeois-
Démocratique Suisse
Conservative Democratic Party

Liberalism

- The economic policy of the **centre-right** favours only **limited State intervention,** without excluding certain social measures, in particular in favour of families. The centre-right is generally opposed to tax increases.

- The **liberal right** favours **very little State intervention** in economic matters and defends the interest of companies. It prefers lowering – even elimination of – certain taxes.

YOU DON'T GET RICH THAT WAY!

Public finance

Public agencies provide services to the population. These services are financed by taxation.

State accounts

Expenditure
The State provides services, such as social insurance, education, health and infrastructure.

Revenue
To finance its activities, the State relies mainly on taxes such as **income tax** or **value-added tax** (VAT).

Budgets

- In Switzerland, public expenditure is at three levels. The **Confederation**, the **cantons** and the **communes** establish a **budget** each year.

- When expenditure is higher than revenue, there is a **budget deficit**. During the 1990 recession public deficits were very high.

- The accounts of public entities follow closely the trend of the economic cycle (⋯⋯ p. 20).

THE TAX RECIPE IS BETTER IF YOU ADD A LITTLE VAT!

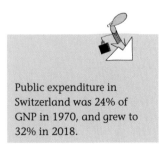

Public expenditure in Switzerland was 24% of GNP in 1970, and grew to 32% in 2018.

Deficits and surpluses in public accounts
(Confederation, cantons, communes and social insurance as % of GNP)

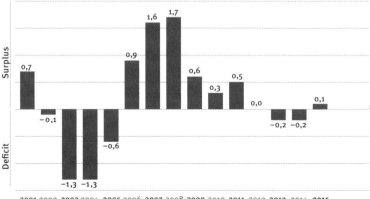

The public debt

- The accumulation of deficits increases public debt. The State invests the money it borrows, thus stimulating **growth**.

  The construction of the Gotthard tunnel increased the federal deficit, but stimulated economic activity for the benefit of many companies and extended communication networks.

- The important thing for the State is to maintain its **capacity for reimbursement**. When debts weigh too heavily on the annual budget, the State must **cut back** expenditure.

- Total public debt (Confederation, cantons and communes) was 190 billion francs in 2018. In 1990, it was 98 billion.

  In 2001, Swiss voters accepted a 'debt brake' that prevents the federal Parliament from voting budgets with high deficits. Several cantons have done the same.

- The **2007–2008 financial crisis** (p. 74) caused a debt crisis around the world.

- The **2020 economic crisis** worsened the public debt situation in almost all countries.

Level of debt
(% of GNP, 2018)

Italy	134.9
Belgium	100.0
France	98.3
Spain	97.6
UK	85.9
Germany	61.8
Sweden	38.7
Switzerland	27.5

Taxation

Taxes are the main source of State revenue. Of every franc raised in taxes, 47 centimes go to the Confederation, 33 to the cantons and 20 to the communes.

In 2018, a single person earning 100,000 francs per year would pay income tax of 20,000 if resident in Delémont (Canton Jura) or 9,000 if resident in Wollerau (Canton Schwyz).

Direct taxes

- make up 70% of Swiss tax revenue;
- are paid directly by physical persons and companies, on the basis of a **tax declaration**;
- are considered **more equitable** than indirect taxes because they vary according to the financial capacity of the taxpayer.

Income tax

Income tax comprises **communal**, **cantonal** and **direct federal** components. The rates are **progressive**, i.e. the higher the income, the higher the percentage of tax levied.

Wealth Tax

Wealth tax is only levied by the cantons and the communes; it applies to total assets of physical persons: **movable goods** (cars, bank balances, etc.) and **real estate** (land and houses, etc.). In most cantons, the tax is progressive.

Company tax (profits and capital)

All companies operating in Switzerland must pay this tax. **Profits** tax is levied at federal, cantonal and communal level. It varies from one location to another (between 16% and 25% in total). Capital tax exists only at cantonal and communal level (between 0.3% and 0.9%).

Withholding tax

This tax is levied at 35% on some forms of income (interest on bank accounts, lottery winnings, etc.). It is reimbursed to the taxpayer when a tax declaration is filed.

Other direct taxes

Taxes are also levied on inheritances, donations, and transfer of real estate.

YOUR EXCELLENCY, YOUR TAX DECLARATION HAS ARRIVED!

↑
WEALTH TAX

↑
INCOME TAX

Indirect taxes

- constitute 30% of tax revenue in Switzerland;

- are **less apparent** to taxpayers because they are integrated in the pricing of goods.

VAT

Value-added tax is the main source of revenue for the Confederation. Currently fixed at 7.7%, VAT is by far the lowest in Europe (20% in France, 25% in Sweden). Some items (food, medicines, newspapers, hotel rooms) benefit from **lower rates** (2.5% or 3.7%).

Customs duties

Duties are levied by the Confederation, mainly on imports of **industrial** and **agricultural** products. They have been substantially reduced through negotiations in the World Trade Organisation (···> p. 82) and have been abolished for products from the European Union and the European Free Trade Association (···> p. 84).

Other indirect taxes

Other indirect taxes fill the public coffers: fuel tax, tobacco tax, automobile tax, dog owners' tax, stamp duty, entertainment tax.

The fiscal autonomy of the cantons

- The cantons are free to levy all taxes that are not specifically reserved to the Confederation.

- The communes may also levy taxes according to the rules laid down by their respective cantonal constitution.

- The cantons and the communes are free to determine their **tax rates**.

> IF YOU STOP SMOKING iT WILL CAUSE GRIEVOUS HARM TO PUBLIC FINANCES!

Some taxes are attributed to precise budgetary objectives, which facilitates their acceptance by the public. For example, tobacco tax is entirely devoted to financing the State old-age and invalidity insurance programmes.

Taxation

Major political debates take place on the subject of taxes. The level of taxes determines the field of action of the State, but also influences its competitivity in relation to other States.

Tax policy

- Taxes **finance State activities** and allow **redistribution of income** in society.

- In Switzerland, income tax is **progressive**: the more you earn, the more tax you pay.

  For example, in the canton of Fribourg, the tax rate on an annual income of 62,000 francs is 9%; on 200,000 it is 13.4%.

- Political parties on the right try to limit or **reduce** taxes.

- Some countries have introduced a so-called '**flat tax**'. It simplifies tax collection, but also goes against the principle of progressivity and solidarity in taxation, by which wealthy people pay a larger proportion of their income in taxes.

IN MY CANTON THEY FLEECED ME.

IN MINE THEY PLUCKED ME CLEAN!

Tax competition

- In Switzerland, the cantons compete on taxes. Some try to attract companies and wealthy taxpayers by offering favourable taxes.

- To a lesser extent, communes also compete on taxation.

Swiss tax rates for companies vary from canton to canton, from 12% to 22%. In Ireland the rate is 12.5%, in France 28%, and in Japan 31%.

Taxes as a percentage of GNP in 2018

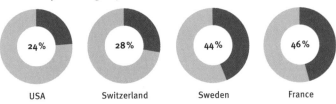

| 24% | 28% | 44% | 46% |
| USA | Switzerland | Sweden | France |

Is Switzerland a tax haven?

For most inhabitants, Switzerland is far from a tax haven. However, for certain companies and individuals, the level of taxation is very low.

- For a long time, as a result of banking secrecy (----} p. 69), Swiss banks used to manage non-declared foreign funds.

  It is estimated that in the early 2000s, more than half of the foreign assets held in Switzerland by foreigners were not declared.

- Today, this phenomenon is much reduced in scope, as a result of the weakening of banking secrecy.

Flat rate taxes for wealthy foreigners

- Many cantons, especially in the French-speaking part of the country, offer **flat-rate all-in taxes** for wealthy foreigners who have no gainful activity here. This taxation method, based on notional **expenses** (not on income) reduces taxation for this group.

- Several cantons have abolished these flat-rate taxes. The Federal Council has tightened the rules applying to flat-rate taxes, making them less attractive.

By offering tax advantages, several small cantons have become tax havens for certain kinds of multinational companies. In Pfäffikon, in the canton of Schwyz, for example, there are dozens of companies specialising in asset management. The town of Baar, in the canton of Zug, is well-known as the domicile for companies trading in raw materials.

Special status of companies

- Until 2019, some companies benefited from a special status that gave them a favourable tax treatment. This was the case for **holding companies** that manage shareholdings in other companies, and so-called *sociétés d'administration*, which have their headquarters in Switzerland but have a purely 'administrative' function and no commercial activity.

- Under pressure from the European Union, Switzerland has been forced to abolish this special treatment and measures to reform company taxation came into force on 1 January 2020.

Unemployment

The unemployment rate is the proportion of persons unemployed in relation to the active population (persons of working age).

Some economists consider that a few percentage points of unemployment are good for the economy. If the supply of jobs was equal to demand (full employment) or even higher, this would increase the cost of labour and thus wages. Maintaining a certain level of unemployment makes it possible to control the cost of production (of which wages are a part).

Different types of unemployment

- **Structural unemployment** affects workers who cannot find work because their skills no longer correspond to the needs of the employment market.

  For example: at the end of the 1980s, most typesetters lost their jobs because their profession had disappeared.

- **Cyclical unemployment** arises when an economy enters recession; production falls and employers lay off staff.

- **Frictional unemployment** affects workers who are unemployed for short periods – between jobs, for example. The frictional unemployment rate is rather low.

- There are many causes of **unemployment**:
  - economic crisis and recession;
  - technological change;
  - productivity improvements (less manpower needed for the same work);
  - change of employment location;
  - population increase.

Tackling unemployment

The State attempts to mitigate unemployment in various ways:
- **lowering of company taxes and social charges** as an incentive to create jobs;
- **investment** to stimulate growth;
- creation of **public employment**;
- **retraining courses** for workers.

Unemployment in Switzerland

Compared with other countries, Swiss unemployment has always been low. In 2019, it was 2.3%, compared with 6.7% in the European Union. Several things explain this special situation.

- Switzerland has specialised in goods with high added value, produced in **small and medium-sized companies**. In Switzerland, layoffs in some of these companies would not create an unemployment crisis.

- The **service** sector, highly developed in Switzerland, has suffered relatively little from the crises affecting the European economy since the 1980s. Periods of recession have thus been less marked, creating less cyclical unemployment than elsewhere on the continent.

  The financial crisis of 2007–2008 and the 'COVID-19' crisis in 2020 have however influenced employment.

- Collective labour agreements (so-called **'labour peace'** ╌╌> p. 48) tend to encourage companies not to implement massive layoffs.

  The unemployment rate does not count beneficiaries of social assistance (who are often without work) or people who have exhausted their State unemployment benefits. There are, moreover, many people who have a job, but who do not earn enough for a decent standard of living (the working poor ╌╌> p. 94).

Unemployment insurance

- Switzerland has a federal unemployment insurance. Employer and employee each contribute 1.1% of wages.

- The unemployed receive 70% to 80% of their previous wage; this varies according to personal circumstances (previous salary level, number of dependents, etc.).

- The maximum level of insured annual earnings is 148,000 francs.

  An unemployed worker whose earnings were higher receives only 70% of this maximum (or 80% in case of dependent children).

- The unemployed can receive up to a maximum of 640 days' daily allowance, dependent on age and length of insurance.

People in independent professions do not pay unemployment insurance. They receive no benefits if they reduce or have to stop their professional activity.

Companies

Legal structures

There are various forms of private companies, of which the most common is the limited company.

Limited companies

In Switzerland, **limited companies** (in French *Société Anonyme SA*, in German *Aktiengesellschaft AG*) are the most common form of commercial organisation. To create a limited company, one or more persons or corporate entities (**shareholders**) must put up at least 100,000 francs (**share capital**).

• The shareholders organise a **General Meeting** (GM), the governing body of the company. Normally the GM meets once a year.

THIS COMPANY IS VERY LIMITED!

• The GM sets up a **Board of directors**, responsible for the governance of the company. The Board appoints a General manager (frequently called a Chief Executive Officer) who is responsible for the day-to-day management.

• Limited companies must submit annual accounts (····> p. 42) for **audit** by an independent body (normally chartered accountants).

• If a limited company cannot reimburse its debts and goes **bankrupt,** the shareholders lose their share capital, but are not liable with their personal assets for company debts.

• Shareholders can sell their shares, the value of which increases or decreases in relation to the value of the company. When a company reaches a certain size, it can request that its shares be traded on a **stock market** (····> p. 70); this makes the shares more widely available and brings in new capital.

When a company goes bankrupt, its assets are sold and its debts reimbursed according to a ranking system. First priority creditors are the employees. If assets remain, they are available for other creditors (for example, suppliers).

Other kinds of companies

Société à responsabilité limitée (SARL)

The SARL is a form of private company that exists mainly in French-speaking countries, including Switzerland (in German *Gesellschaft mit beschränkter Haftung* GmbH). Formation of a SARL requires less capital than a SA (at least 20,000 francs), but its shares cannot be traded on the stock market and are less easily transferable. In case of bankruptcy, the owners are only liable up to the amount they have contributed to the company's capital.

Partnerships

- In Switzerland **Société en nom collectif**, **société en commandite simple** and **société simple** (in German *Kollektivgesellschaft*, *Kommanditgesellschaft* and *Einfache Gesellschaft*) are forms of partnership that are easy to set up, but the partners are personally liable. In case of bankruptcy they are responsible for the company's debts.

- **Entreprises individuelles** ('personal' companies, in German *Einzelunternehmen*) are also very easy to set up and are the most widespread type of company in Switzerland. Independent (freelance) contractors belong to this category.

DON'T SHOUT
AT THE OWNER
- HIS WIFE
DOES THAT.

Cooperatives

Cooperatives are set up primarily for the benefit of their members (for example, farmers may create a cooperative for cheese-processing). The members may make financial contributions that constitute the cooperative's capital.

Associations

Associations are not complicated to set up, but cannot engage in profit-making activity. They are not appropriate for trading and sales.

Foundations

A foundation can employ assets (for example, an inheritance) for a specific purpose that cannot subsequently be changed. A federal agency supervises foundations to ensure that their assets are used in conformity with their statutes.

In Switzerland, some very large companies, such as Raiffeisen Bank, la Mobilière (insurance), Coop and Migros, have taken the form of cooperatives. Migros has more than 2 million associates who each have a 'share' of 10 francs – but this share cannot be sold.

Companies large and small

Switzerland is home to several hundred multinational companies, some of which are among the largest in the world – but two thirds of employees in Switzerland work in small and medium-sized companies.

The Swiss newspaper *Handelszeitung* collects statistical data on 1300 companies in 80 different economic areas. This information is used for an annual ranking of the largest companies in the country, published in August.

Large companies

A large company is defined as one with more than 250 employees; they represent 0.4% of all companies based in Switzerland, but employ one third of the active work force.

Industry, trade and services
(Turnover in billion francs, 2019)

1. **Vitol**	raw material trading	223.7
2. **Glencore**	raw material trading	213.8
3. **Trafigura**	raw material trading	170.5
4. **Mercuria**	raw material trading	115.3
5. **Cargill**	raw material trading	112.8
6. **Nestlé**	agri-food	92.6
7. **Gunvor**	raw material trading	74.6
8. **Roche**	chemicals/pharmaceuticals	63.8
9. **Novartis**	chemicals/pharmaceuticals	47.2
10. **BHP Billiton**	raw material trading	44.0

Banks
(Total assets* in billion francs, 2019)

1. **UBS**	966.3
2. **Credit Suisse**	792.0
3. **Raiffeisen Group**	248.3
4. **Zurich Kantonalbank**	167.1
5. **Postfinance**	125.6

Insurance
(Gross premium income* in billion francs, 2015)

1. **Zurich**	47.8
2. **Swiss Re**	42.0
3. **Swiss Life**	23.0
4. **Baloise**	9.5
5. **Helvetia**	9.2

*Turnover is not relevant in measuring banking and insurance activity; these two sectors have their own indicators.

WE ARE IN THE FOOD BUSINESS, WE SWALLOW EVERYTHING THAT COMES OUR WAY!

Small and medium-sized companies

- **Small and medium-sized companies** are defined by the fact that they have less than 250 employees.

- They comprise **99.6%** of all companies in Switzerland.

- They employ **67%** of the active Swiss workforce.

- **87%** of them have less than 10 employees (**micro-enterprises**).

- **Independent contractors/Freelance workers** are also included in this category.

- Small and medium-sized companies are the backbone of the Swiss economy.

> In 2019, the biggest private employer in Switzerland was Coop, with 78,264 employees; Migros was second, with 75,606.

Business associations

- **Economiesuisse** is the central federation of Swiss companies. It has some 100,000 members and defends business freedom and free market principles.

- The **Swiss Employers Confederation** (*Union patronale suisse*) brings together some 80 employers' organisations.

  For example, Swiss Hotel Association, Swiss Brewing Association, Union of Swiss Chocolate Manufacturers, Swiss Cigarette, Swiss Food Industries

COMPANY FORMATION

OH, IF ONLY I COULD HAVE MY OWN COMPANY!

OH, IF ONLY I COULD TAKE SOMEONE ON TO DO MY WORK!

PHASE 1

PHASE 2

Entrepreneurs

Switzerland owes a large part of its prosperity to a few visionaries who were pioneers in their respective fields.

A GRATEFUL NATION

Some other well-known names:
- Philippe Suchard (1797–1884), chocolate manufacturer;
- Carl Franz Bally (1821–1899), shoe manufacturer;
- Rudolf Lindt (1855–1909), chocolate manufacturer;
- Albert Wander (1867–1950), inventor of Ovomaltine/Ovaltine;
- Fritz Hoffmann-La Roche (1868–1920), pharmaceutical manufacturer;
- Louis Chevrolet (1878–1941), car manufacturer.

Some personalities

- **Henri Nestlé** (1814–1890) was born in Frankfurt and emigrated to Switzerland in 1833. He settled in Vevey, where he invented milk powder – a product that enjoyed enormous success throughout Europe. The **Nestlé** empire grew with the acquisition of other Swiss companies, including those founded by François-Louis Cailler (1796–1852) and Julius Maggi (1846–1912).

- **Alfred Escher** (1819–1882) is considered to be one of the founding fathers of modern Switzerland. An industrialist and politician from Zurich, he participated in drafting the first federal Constitution in 1848, fought for railway construction, founded **Credit Suisse** and set up the first insurance company (Rentenanstalt, later **Swiss Life**).

- **César Ritz** (1850–1918) was the pioneer of the luxury hotel business. Born in Niederwald (canton of Valais), he opened his first hotel in Paris in 1898, before extending his empire to other capital cities, such as London and Madrid. Today there are **Ritz-Carlton** hotels in the major cities of the world.

- **Édouard Sandoz** (1853–1928) and **Alfred Kern** (1850–1893) founded a chemical company in 1886 that specialised in dyes. In 1917, the company moved into pharmaceutical research and developed the first psychotropic drugs (including LSD, invented in the Sandoz laboratories in 1938). In 1996, Sandoz merged with Ciba-Geigy to form the giant **Novartis**.

- **Gottlieb Duttweiler** (1888–1962) founded **Migros** in 1925. With five Ford Model-T trucks, he criss-crossed Switzerland and sold his products directly to consumers, bypassing intermediaries. He became both wholesaler ('*grossiste*') and retailer, hence the name Migros. By combining quality and low prices, Migros became number one in the retail trade in Switzerland.

- **Henri-Ferdinand Lavanchy** (1926–2012) created a temporary employment agency in Lausanne in 1957, better known as **Adia Interim**. He was one of the inventors of temporary work, a business that enjoyed enormous success in the second half of the 20th century. Today, the company has become **Adecco**, the world leader in temporary work.

- **Nicolas Hayek** (1928–2010) contributed to the rescue of the Swiss watch industry during the 1970s. In 1980, he brought out the *Swatch*, a simple and cheap watch, sold as a fashion accessory. Today, the **Swatch Group** is the largest watch-making company in the world and owns the prestigious names of Bréguet, Blancpain, Longines and Omega.

Future Trends

High tech

Swiss companies are world leaders in several areas, including **packaging** machinery (Alupack) and **machine tools** (Bobst). Thanks to state-of-the-art knowledge in high tech, several Swiss companies are engaged in futuristic projects, such as advanced **medical technology** (Medtronic), or **semiconductor** production (EM Microelectronic).

Thanks to nanotechnology, STMicroelectronics, in Geneva, has designed accelerometers for the Nintendo Wii console. These chips react to the minutest change of direction or speed.

Information technology

This vast sector encompasses all the companies active in information processing and transmission. Logitech, founded in Apples (canton of Vaud) in 1981, is a major manufacturer of **peripheral computer devices** (mouse, keyboard, webcam, etc.). Another group in Vaud is **Kudelski**, one of the world leaders in **digital security**.

Biotechnology

One of the key areas of the **life sciences**, biotechnology is used primarily in agriculture, food and medicine. Syngenta in Basel is one of the largest companies in this sector.

Nanotechnology

Nanotechnology relates to the production of highly miniaturised structures, at the scale of a nanometre (a billionth of a metre). It relates to areas as varied as electronics, engineering, medicine, defence, aerospace or cosmetics. The federal technical universities, EPFL and ETHZ, are among the principal research resources for nanotechnology.

Company accounting

The balance sheet is a 'photograph' of the financial situation of a company at a given moment. It is drawn up at the end of each accounting period, normally the 31st of December.

The balance sheet

There are two parts to a balance sheet: the assets (what the company owns) and the liabilities (how the company finances what it owns).

For example:
The COMYXY company publishes comic books. Here is its balance sheet at 31 December 2019:

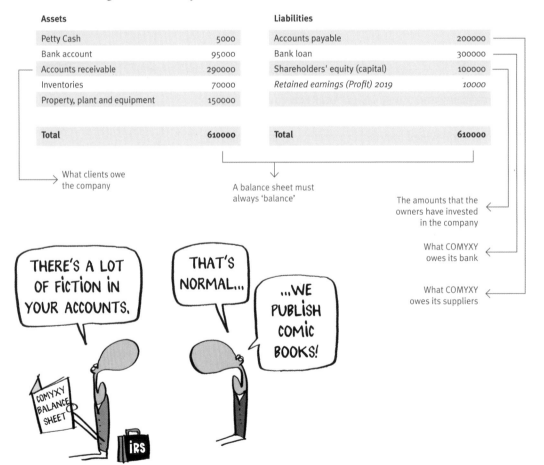

Balance sheet 31 December 2019

Assets		Liabilities	
Petty Cash	5000	Accounts payable	200000
Bank account	95000	Bank loan	300000
Accounts receivable	290000	Shareholders' equity (capital)	100000
Inventories	70000	*Retained earnings (Profit) 2019*	*10000*
Property, plant and equipment	150000		
Total	**610000**	**Total**	**610000**

What clients owe the company

A balance sheet must always 'balance'

The amounts that the owners have invested in the company

What COMYXY owes its bank

What COMYXY owes its suppliers

THERE'S A LOT OF FICTION IN YOUR ACCOUNTS.

THAT'S NORMAL...

...WE PUBLISH COMIC BOOKS!

COMYXY BALANCE SHEET

IRS

What the balance sheet shows

- COMYXY's accounts show a **profit** of 10,000 francs at the end of 2019. The shareholders decide to pay out no dividends (i.e. they leave the profits in the company, as reinvestment). The shareholders' equity (share capital and profit) will be 110,000 francs on 1st January 2020.

- Even if the total assets are 610,000 francs, the **value** of COMYXY (own funds) is only 110,000 francs. This normal, because the company has debts of 500,000 francs (accounts payable and bank loan).

- COMYXY has a high level of **debt**. This means that the company must generate profits in order to pay off its bank loan and improve its autonomy.

- COMYXY's **liquidity** (petty cash and bank account) is unfavourable. If its clients (accounts receivable) do not pay their bills in time, COMIXY will not have enough liquid funds to pay its own suppliers (accounts payable).

- The **balance sheet structure** is not good, because the plant and equipment are partly financed by short-term debts (accounts payable and bank loan). If the debts had to be paid rapidly, COMYXY would have to sell off part of its property, plant and equipment, putting the operation of the company in danger.

SHORT RECKONINGS MAKE LONG FRIENDS,

A PROVERB INVENTED BY CREDITORS!

Company accounting

The earnings report

The earnings report summarises all the income and expenditure for the year.

The earnings report (also called the **profit and loss account**) shows the company result for a given period (profit or loss).

For example:
The COMYXY company published three new albums in 2019.

Earnings report for the period 1 January to 31 December 2019

Expenditure		Income	
Raw materials	100000	Sales of Album 1	250000
Printing costs	150000	Sales of Album 2	180000
Marketing/sales costs	40000	Sales of Album 3	140000
Personnel costs	200000		
Rent	40000		
Overhead expenses and amortisation	30000		
Profit	*10000*		
Total	**570000**	**Total (turnover)**	**570000**

If income is higher than expenditure, there is a profit

The earnings report must always balance

Amortisation is the loss of value of certain assets on the balance sheet

A KID CALLED TINTIN WITH A LITTLE WHITE DOG?

THAT WILL NEVER MAKE A PROFIT!

What the earnings report shows:

- COMYXY sold albums for a total of 570,000 francs in 2019: this is its **turnover**.

- COMYXY had an excess of income over expenditure of 10,000 francs in 2019: this is its profit.

- The result is the difference between expenditure and income. In the case of profit, the amount is included under expenditure; in the case of loss, under income.

Public companies

Broadly speaking, all companies owned by the State are considered as public. They come in a variety of legal forms, from associations to limited companies. Some are based on private law, others are created by a specific law and are thus based on public law.

Public service

- Public service comprises all services provided by the State in the **general interest** of the population.

- In addition to public administration (for example, federal and cantonal offices), dozens of companies under State control work in the interests of society.

  If a company such as the Swiss railways (CFF/SBB/FFS) was owned privately, only the most profitable lines would be kept open. It is considered in the general interest that the State should own the railways, in order to guarantee a satisfactory transport infrastructure.

Privatisation and deregulation

- Since the 1990s, globalisation, opening up of markets and European integration, have led the Federal Council to deregulate certain sectors.

- Opening markets to foreign competition ended some **State monopolies**, in particular in telecommunications.

  Before the liberalisation of telecom services in 1998, Swisscom (previously PTT) benefited from a State monopoly. The arrival of competing firms led to a fall in prices and stimulated innovation.

- When the State withdraws from a company, it is called **privatisation**. In recent years, privatisation of Swisscom has been discussed; the Confederation would sell a sufficient proportion of its shares so that it would no longer be the majority shareholder. The political left is opposed to this because it fears that peripheral regions would no longer get adequate service.

Swissair was frequently referred to as the national airline, but the State never had a controlling interest. When the company went bankrupt in 2001, the Confederation held only 3% of the capital. Since the purchase of the new company Swiss by Lufthansa in 2005, the Confederation has no shareholding in the civil air transport sector.

Some public companies

La Poste

The disappearance of the PTT in 1998 gave birth to a new independent institution, La Poste. It is entirely in the hands of the Confederation and is required to fulfil a public service in delivering **mail and parcels** and providing **payment** services and **public transport**.

Since 2004, the postal market has been partly liberalised and La Poste no longer has a monopoly for deliveries above a certain weight; since 2009, this limit is fixed at 50 grammes.

The cantons and communes also have their own public companies: transport, industrial services, cantonal banks and some hospitals. The Geneva international airport is a public company owned 100% by the canton. The Zurich airport, on the other hand, is a limited company listed on the stock exchange; the town of Zurich holds 5% of the capital and the canton 33%.

Swisscom

Swisscom is a limited company that took over the **telecommunications** activities of the PTT. The Confederation holds 51% of the shares. Swisscom has a legal obligation to provide **universal service**: it must provide telephone lines to the whole population in all regions of Switzerland.

The federal railways

The federal railways were set up in 1902 by nationalising the main private railway companies of the time. In 1999, the company lost its status as a federal agency and became a limited company. The Confederation holds all the shares.

Swiss radio and television

The SSR (Swiss radio and television) is an association with a public service mandate. It comprises different entities, such as the French-speaking radio and TV (RTS) and the German-speaking radio and TV (SRF). It is financed by compulsory fees levied on private households by the company Serafe.

Some other public companies are: Swiss Tourism, ProHelvetia (Swiss foundation for culture), Ruag (armaments industry), and the Swiss National Park.

ALL THE ANIMALS HERE ARE PROTECTED SPECIES... THEY ARE STATE EMPLOYEES!

SWISS NATIONAL PARK

The trade unions

Trade unions exist to defend the interests of workers. In Switzerland, they are important economic actors, because they participate in the negotiation of collective labour agreements that determine, among other things, the level of wages.

The role of trade unions

- Unions appeared in Europe in the 19th century. Workers united to improve their negotiating position vis-à-vis **employers**.

- The unions have three main demands: length of **working hours**, **wages** and **working conditions**.

- Action by unions includes negotiation, demonstrations, strikes (recognised by the federal constitution since 1999), initiation of referenda or political initiatives, and media publication. Unions are consulted in the drafting of laws.

In Switzerland, some 740,000 workers belong to a union, 15% of the active population. In France, the figure is 8%, in the USA 11% and in Sweden 68%.

Collective bargaining

- The unions negotiate collective labour agreements with the employers. These agreements determine minimum wages and general working conditions in each branch of the economy. Working hours and minimum wages are not the subject of any Swiss law.

12 million workers are covered by collective agreements in Switzerland.

- Most collective agreements include provisions for 'labour peace'; all labour conflicts must be settled by negotiation and, in principle, strikes are excluded. 'Labour peace' has existed in Switzerland since 1937.

The main Swiss unions

In Switzerland, most unions belong to one of two main groupings.

- **USS** (*Union syndicale suisse*), founded in 1880, comprises 388,000 members and 16 unions, among which:
  - **Unia**, formed through a merger between the SIB (industry and building), FMTH (metalworking and watch-making) and FCTA (trade, transport and food) 200,000 members;
  - **SEV** (transport), 43,000 members;
  - **SSP** (public transport), 35,000 members;
  - **Syndicom** (media and communication), 34,000 members.

- **Travail.Suisse**, founded in 2002 by a merger of the CSC (Christian unions) and FSE (employees' associations), has about 150,000 members and includes the following main unions:
  - **Syna** (artisans, industry and services);
  - **OCST** (Christian Social union of the canton of Ticino);
  - **Employés Suisse** (mechanical engineering, chemical and pharmaceutical industries);
  - **SCIV** (Christian unions of the canton of Valais);
  - **Transfair** (public sector and services);
  - **Hotel & Gastro Union** (hotels and restaurants).

Some unions do not belong to either grouping; this includes the unions for the teaching profession, communal and cantonal employees, and the SEC (commercial employees), with 55,000 members.

Switzerland is not very much affected by strikes. In the last 25 years, the country has never had more than 10 per year. Among major recent labour conflicts, the one at the company Swissmetal in Reconvilier (canton of Bern) attracted the most attention. It lasted a month, from 25 January to 24 February 2006.

Markets

Supply and demand

The law of supply and demand determines the price and the quantity of any given commodity or service traded on a market.

NOT TODAY, THANK YOU!!

Cigarettes are a product for which demand is inelastic. Price increases do not significantly influence the quantity sold. To reduce demand for cigarettes, (and tobacco consumption), the State can only increase the price through taxation. The State can also encourage changes in consumer behaviour, by campaigns to raise awareness of the dangers of smoking, for example.

Markets

- In the beginning, markets were places where producers and consumers met physically for **trading** products.

- The current notion of market is more **abstract**, although the basic reasoning is the same. There is a market for each product category.

  For example: telecommunications market, textile market

- The market price of a good or service is determined by **supply** and **demand**.

Supply

- Supply is the **quantity** of goods and services that producers are willing to **sell** at a given market **price**.

- If the price increases, the quantity supplied goes up, because suppliers want to increase their **profit**. Conversely, if the price goes down, the quantity goes down too.

Demand

- Demand is the **quantity** of goods and services that consumers are prepared to **buy** at a given market **price**.

- Demand can be more or less **'elastic'**:
  - demand for goods for which there are readily available substitutes is very elastic, because variations in price have a great influence on the quantity consumed;

    For example: if there is big increase in the price of sunflower oil, consumption will drop heavily because consumers can replace it with peanut oil, a virtually identical product.
  - demand for goods that **cannot easily be substituted** is inelastic, because the price does have much effect on the quantity consumed.

    For example: if the price of salt goes up, the quantity consumed will not go down, because salt is a basic commodity product (it cannot be replaced by another product).

Trend of price and traded quantity for a product with average elasticity of supply and demand: denim jeans

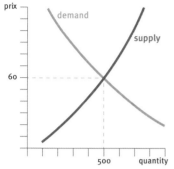

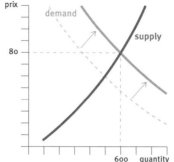

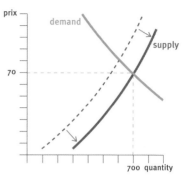

The price and quantity of jeans traded are shown by the intersection of the two curves. At 60 francs, 500 jeans are sold.

***Fashion** trends increase demand for jeans. Price and quantity rise. Producers make more in order to increase their profit.*

***Technological innovation** allows producers to lower production costs and offer lower prices. Quantity sold increases and the price falls.*

The limits of the theory

- The law of supply and demand, one of the fundamental elements of the **capitalist** system, is very theoretical:
  - it supposes that purchasers and producers all seek to gain the maximum **profit**;
  - the act of purchasing may, however, be motivated by other, less rational motives;
  - for the law to apply, the market must be entirely **free and transparent**; **competition** (····⟩ p. 54) must be perfect, in order to allow consumers to have **free** choice of products at the lowest prices, and **State intervention** must be **limited**.

- Very few markets are entirely free and transparent:
  - State intervention, even if it is minimal, is always present through **taxes** and **subsidies**;

    For example: in Switzerland, agricultural products are not sold at real market prices. Subsidies are applied to bring their price down artificially. Without these, agriculture would disappear, because producers could not offer their products at prices that compete with foreign products.

  - several **laws** oblige producers to respect certain standards; this increases the cost – and thus the price – of some goods.

    For example: clean-air standards make cars more expensive.

- Many consumers do not view price as the sole argument for buying a product.

  For example: in Switzerland, fair-trade bananas are more expensive but sell better than other bananas.

In contrast to free markets, there are planned markets. This was the case in the USSR, where the prices of products and services were not determined by supply and demand, but by the State. One of the main defects of planned markets is the risk of shortages (supply does not automatically adapt to demand): there were long queues outside Soviet food shops.

Competition

Competition allows producers to offer freely their goods and services in a market. It also allows purchasers to choose freely between these goods and services. The principle of competition is at the heart of the market economy.

In theory

For perfect competition, several factors must be present.

- State intervention must be very limited. The State must only set up a **general framework** that guarantees the principle of private property and ensures respect for the rules of competition.

- The market must be sufficiently **broad**. In order for there to be a genuine **choice**, there must be a large number of purchasers and sellers.

- Information must be **freely** available. It must circulate widely and be transparent enough to allow comparison between products.

- The **products** sold in a market must be sufficiently **similar** to permit price comparison.

- Purchasers and sellers must have **free access** to the whole market.

  The stock market is the only one with almost perfect competition.

Advantages

- Competition stimulates **innovation**. Producers develop new products in order to be a step ahead of their competitors.

- Competition leads to **lower prices**. If a company makes enormous profits in a market, this encourages others to offer similar products at a lower price.

  The arrival of hard discounters (Aldi, Lidl) on the Swiss market forced the main supermarkets to reduce their margins and offer a range of lower-priced products (M-Budget by Migros, Prix Garantie by Coop, and others).

In Switzerland, competition has diminished in certain sectors. In the retail trade, for example, two groups have taken over several of their competitors: Coop acquired Waro and EPA; Migros bought Globus and Denner, the latter having already taken over Pick Pay.

Imperfect competition

There are several constraints on competition.

- When one or more companies have a predominant position that enables them to fix prices freely, this is known as a **monopoly** or an **oligopoly**.

  For example: Microsoft holds approximately 90% of the market for computer operating systems.

- When companies reach agreement to fix prices, quantities produced or market shares for each, in order to avoid mutual competition, this is known as a **cartel**. In Switzerland, cartels are, in principle, illegal.

  Until 1991, the Swiss beer market was dominated by a cartel. Its disappearance led to a lowering of prices and allowed other breweries to gain a foothold in the national market.

- There are sometimes **unwritten agreements** between companies. They are similar to cartels but, because they are informal, are much more difficult to prove.

- **Patents** issued by the State protect a product, in the country of issue, against competition for several years (in Switzerland, for a maximum of 20 years). Patented products must be innovative.

  For example: after the expiry of the patent on aspirin, several pharmaceutical companies developed a generic version, which they sold at a lower price.

- State **subsidies** for certain companies allow them to lower their prices and give them an advantage over their competitors.

- Sometimes **quality standards** are enforced by **law** – these prevent entry of some products to the market. Product labelling, that protects certain products, can also be imposed by law.

  For example: certification of origin (appellation d'origine protégée – AOP) for raclette cheese prohibits producers of similar cheese products from another region (other than the canton of Valais) from selling their product under the name 'raclette'.

- The State may also, for reasons of public policy, protect some markets from competition.

  For example: health, education, culture

In Switzerland, companies found guilty of cartel collusion or abuse of a dominant market position are subject to a fine of up to 10% of their turnover. In 2012, the Competition Commission (COMCO), that supervises the application of anti-cartel law, found the German car manufacturer BMW guilty of restricting direct and parallel importation of its vehicles into Switzerland – the company was fined 156 million francs.

Prices

Prices vary according to supply and demand. They are also influenced by legislative and regulatory measures.

One can estimate price differences between countries using the *Big Mac* as a measure. It is the same everywhere and therefore an easily comparable product. Moreover, the different ingredients (meat, bread, labour, etc.) are a good indication of the prices in each country. In 2020, the price of a *Big Mac* was:
CHF 6.90 in Zurich
CHF 5.80 in New York
CHF 5.50 in London
CHF 3.40 in Tokyo
CHF 3.00 in Beijing

Price Index

- The Swiss consumer price index (*indice suisse des prix à la consommation* – IPC/*Landesindex der Konsumentenpreise* – LIK) is calculated on the basis of a standard **'basket'** of goods and services.

- Each category of goods and services is **weighted** so as to reflect the consumption of an average household.

- The IPC is the basis for calculating the **rate of inflation** (┄┄⟩ p. 58)

- It also allows measurement of the increase in price of a given commodity for a defined period.

  For example: the price of television sets fell by 32% between 2015 and 2020.

Composition and weighting of the standard 'basket' in 2020

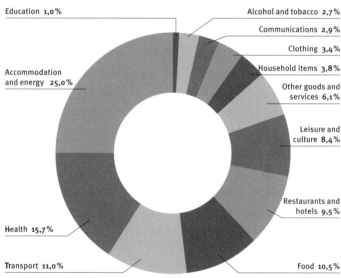

Education 1,0%
Alcohol and tobacco 2,7%
Communications 2,9%
Clothing 3,4%
Household items 3,8%
Accommodation and energy 25,0%
Other goods and services 6,1%
Leisure and culture 8,4%
Restaurants and hotels 9,5%
Health 15,7%
Transport 11,0%
Food 10,5%

THAT'S EXPENSIVE!

WE'RE NOT IN NEW YORK!

Mc ZÜRI

The 'high price island'

- Switzerland is the most expensive country in Europe. The government tries to fight this phenomenon by allowing free rein to the law of supply and demand.

- The **Competition Commission** (Comco) is responsible for ensuring observance of the law on cartels and preventing unjustified price increases.

- Price monitoring is undertaken by a government service, the head of which is known familiarly as **Monsieur Prix** ('Mr. Price'), that denounces abusive pricing in cases where competition is limited (monopolies, administered prices).

> QUICK, MARK IT DOWN TO 12, HERE COMES MR. PRICE!

- The **deregulation** of some highly protected markets leads to a fall in prices.

Thanks to the deregulation of the telecom market, the price of a one-minute telephone conversation between Switzerland and the USA fell from 1 franc in 1992 to less than 10 centimes today.

- **Parallel imports** allow the Swiss to purchase some products abroad (such as cars), bypassing official distributors and resulting in a fall in prices.

- A trade policy measure known as **Cassis de Dijon** (····> p. 85), effective since 2010, allows products legally authorised for the European market to circulate freely in Switzerland, even if they have been produced according to standards or quality requirements different from those applicable in Switzerland.

Price monitoring (*Monsieur Prix – Mr. Price*) was implemented as a result of a vote initiated by the Swiss people ('initiative populaire') in 1982.

Inflation

The rate of inflation is the annual percentage increase in the consumer price index.

Interest rates are related indirectly to inflation. Money put into a bank account in Turkey in Turkish *lira* attracts a higher rate of interest than in Switzerland, but risks a drop in value because the *lira* is subject to higher inflation than the Swiss franc.

Stability at any price

- When the **overall price level goes up,** the purchasing power of a currency declines. This is called **inflation.**

- A slight annual increase in prices is normal. In Switzerland, annual inflation **below 2%** is considered a factor of stability.

- However, high inflation **impoverishes the whole population** of a country, because the currency goes down in value.

- Inflation depends on a number of factors. A distinction is made between:
  - **demand** inflation;
    For example: a rapidly growing economy creates demand for products and services and pushes prices up.
  - **cost** inflation;
    For example: an oil shock provokes a generalised increase in prices, because many companies suffer the consequences.

- If the rate of inflation drops below 0% for a relatively long period, this is known as **deflation.**

  Deflation is just as bad as inflation. If everyone expects prices to fall, it makes sense to postpone purchasing for the moment. In this way, investment and consumption are frozen.

Rate of inflation in Switzerland

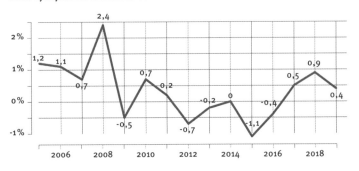

The fight against inflation

- The Central Bank of each country or monetary zone attempts to combat inflation and deflation.

- In Switzerland, the Swiss National Bank (SNB) fulfils this role (⋯⋯> p. 64).

  Such measures only take effect after two or three years. The Central Bank must attempt to foresee probable developments in the economy and act sufficiently early.

Typical scenario of anti-inflationary measures

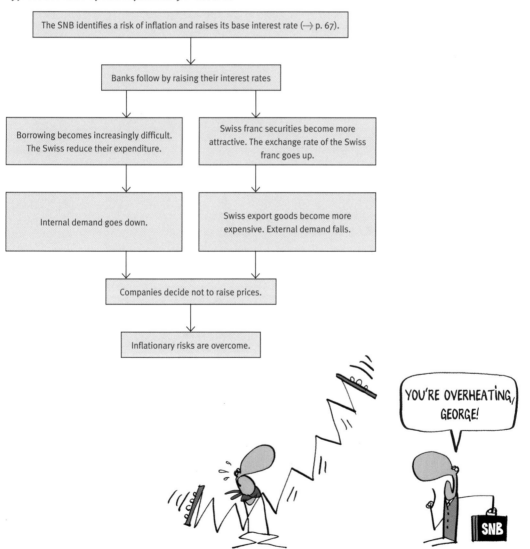

The SNB identifies a risk of inflation and raises its base interest rate (⋯⋯> p. 67).

Banks follow by raising their interest rates

Borrowing becomes increasingly difficult. The Swiss reduce their expenditure.

Swiss franc securities become more attractive. The exchange rate of the Swiss franc goes up.

Internal demand goes down.

Swiss export goods become more expensive. External demand falls.

Companies decide not to raise prices.

Inflationary risks are overcome.

YOU'RE OVERHEATING, GEORGE!

SNB

Finance

Currency

The currency facilitates economic transactions. It exists as cash and bank money (deposits).

A means of exchange

- Currency is an instrument for **trade** and **payment**.

  In a barter system, a seller who wanted to exchange his surplus of rice for a sheep had first to find a partner for the transaction. The introduction of currency solved this problem.

- Currency is also a medium for **savings**, since it can be kept without fear of deterioration.

- Currency can take different forms, provided each is **commonly accepted** and everyone has confidence in its value.

  In the past, shells, animal teeth, precious stones and metals, such as gold and silver, have all been forms of currency. During World War II, in prisoner-of-war camps, cigarettes served as currency.

- Nowadays, currency exists mainly as **cash** (coins and notes) and **deposits** (bank/postal accounts or electronic money).

Swiss banknotes in circulation (2019)

Denomination	Quantity
10 francs	79 million
20 francs	92 million
50 francs	68 million
100 francs	135 million
200 francs	67 million
500 francs	0,2 million
1000 francs	47 million

The Swiss franc

- The Swiss franc was introduced in **1850**. Prior to that, each canton and large town had its own money, and several foreign coins were also in circulation.

- Since 1907, Swiss bank notes are issued by the central bank (**SNB** ⋯⋟ p. 64)

  In 1870, 28 different banks issued notes in Switzerland.

- Coins are minted by the **Swissmint** company, part of the federal Finance Department.

- The official abbreviation of the Swiss franc is CHF (Confœderatio Helvetica Franc).

THE SWISS FRANC DOESN'T STINK!

Foreign currency

- Most national currencies (foreign currency) are **traded freely** on foreign exchange markets, on the basis of supply and demand.

- The central bank can influence the **exchange rate** by buying or selling large quantities of foreign currency or by changing the interest rate it charges banks (····⟩ p. 67).

- If the Swiss franc exchange rate rises, Swiss currency **appreciates** in value and Swiss export products are more expensive.

  For example: when the value of the Swiss franc goes up against the Euro, the Swiss tourist sector worries about a fall in hotel occupancy, because European tourists have to pay more Euros for their stay.

- If the Swiss franc falls, the currency **depreciates**. Swiss export products become cheaper, but imported products are more expensive for Swiss consumers.

Some preconceptions

- A currency is neither weak nor strong in the absolute; it is more or less strong relative to another currency over a given period.

  For example: between early 2014 and end-2015, the exchange rate of the Euro went from CHF 1.23 to CHF 1.08; the Swiss franc became stronger against the Euro. During the same period, the dollar rate went from CHF 0.90 to CHF 1.00; the Swiss franc weakened against the dollar.

- Exchange rates are no indication of the cost of living in a country.

  For example: London is certainly an expensive city, but this has no relation to the exchange rate of the pound (approx. CHF 1.20). As further proof, Tokyo is also an expensive city, but 1 yen is worth less than one Swiss centime.

When the value of a currency becomes unstable, it creates uncertainty and people turn to another currency. During the armed conflicts in ex-Yugoslavia in the 1990s, the Deutschmark was used instead of the Dinar.

The Swiss National Bank

The Swiss National Bank implements the country's monetary policy by regulating the money supply.

In the past, central banks were obliged to keep a certain amount of gold in their vaults to guarantee the value of their currency. This rule, known as the gold standard, was gradually abandoned at the end of the 20th century. Switzerland was the last country to drop the gold standard (in 2000). Some economists and politicians argue for the reintroduction of the gold standard to prevent the central banks from issuing too much money.

Mission

- As in most countries, Switzerland has a **central bank**, the **Swiss National Bank** (SNB).

  In the USA, the central bank is the Federal Reserve (also known as 'the Fed'). In the UK, it is the Bank of England. In Europe, central banks of the Euro-zone countries have delegated their powers to the European Central Bank (ECB).

- The SNB has the **exclusive right to issue** banknotes in Switzerland. It has full **independence** in its work, but is accountable to the political authorities.

- The cantons and the cantonal banks hold a majority of its shares, but some are held by private investors. The Confederation is not a shareholder.

  When the SNB makes a profit, two-thirds are paid out to the cantons and a third to the Confederation.

The money supply

- The central bank issues banknotes and lends to the commercial banks. This creates the **monetary base**.

- Commercial banks lend to households and companies, creating 'invisible' **bank money**. This adds to the monetary base and forms the money supply in the wide sense of the term.

  - The State is not allowed to use the central bank to finance public expenditure.

  - When a central bank increases the money supply, it is sometimes called **'printing money'**. In reality, the number of banknotes does not increase; the new money is bank money.

    As a concrete example, if the SNB buys dollars from a commercial bank, no banknotes change hands – a credit is booked to the bank's deposit account with the SNB. It has exactly the same effect as if the central bank 'printed money'.

Monetary policy

- Under the federal constitution, the SNB is required to follow a policy that is in the **general interest** of the country.

- The SNB must ensure price stability by controlling inflation (····﹥ p. 58). For this purpose, it attempts to make appropriate adjustments to the money supply.

  In theory, the central bank of a country can issue as much money as it wishes. In practice, excessive amounts lead inevitably to inflation, thereby devaluing all the money in circulation.

- The SNB manages the money supply by influencing interest rates (····﹥ p. 67).

  It also uses other mechanisms such as foreign exchange operations.

The franc versus the euro

- From 2009, the debt crisis in the eurozone (····﹥ p. 77) incited many investors to buy Swiss francs as a **safe haven**. The franc appreciated in relation to other currencies, which created serious problems for Swiss exporters.

  Between January 2010 and August 2011, the euro/CHF exchange rate fell from CHF 1.47 to CHF 1.10. The SNB attempted to weaken the franc by massive purchases of euros (more than 100 billion), but the strategy failed.

- On 6 September 2011, the SNB made a historic announcement: the introduction of a 'floor price' (minimum exchange rate). It committed to take all necessary measures (including unlimited expansion of the money supply) to guarantee a minimum euro exchange rate of CHF 1.20.

  In 1978, the SNB made a similar decision by announcing a floor price of 80 centimes for the German mark. The measure was successful, but, in the medium term, led to high inflation (6.5% in 1981 and 5.7% in 1982).

- On 15 January 2015, the SNB abandoned its floor price policy because it considered that the overpricing of the Swiss franc was within reasonable bounds. Since then, the euro rate has been in the range CHF 1.05–1.15.

In January 2012, a political scandal forced the President of the SNB, Philipp Hildebrand, to resign. He had allowed his wife to undertake several important foreign currency transactions prior to the introduction of the floor price. This potential conflict of interest seriously harmed the reputation of the President, who had to resign his position in order to safeguard the credibility of the SNB.

Banks

The banking sector represents 5% of GNP and employs 3.5% of the total workforce.

The cantonal banks are fully or partly owned by the cantons. Solothurn and Appenzell Ausserrhoden have no cantonal bank: the former cantonal banks in these two cantons got into financial difficulties in the 1990s, and their operations were taken over by the Société de Banque Suisse and the Union de Banques Suisses before the two merged in 1998 to become UBS.

The role of banking

- Banks are financial intermediaries that make available **clients' savings to borrowers**.
- Companies and individuals can obtain a **loan** to finance their activities; loans are subject to **interest** payments.
- Banks also offer **financial services** such as **payments** (e.g. settling of bills, money transfers).

There are hundreds of banks

- The two **big banks** in Switzerland, UBS and Credit Suisse, provide approximately half of the jobs in the sector.
- There are 24 **cantonal banks**; they support the local economy by providing loans.

  For some years now they have been increasingly engaged in real estate and wealth management.

- The total includes **60 regional and independent savings banks**, as well as the Raiffeisen bank group, which comprises 246 banks with 896 small co-operative agencies. With online, commercial, private and foreign banks, Switzerland has **246 banking institutions**.

Supervisory authority

- The **Finma** (Swiss Financial Market Supervisory Authority) ensures protection of depositors and enforces compliance with banking laws. It is also the supervisory authority for insurance companies.
- Finma's Executive Board is appointed by the Federal Council. It is financed by the institutions it supervises.

Interest rates

- The SNB provides funds to the banks in the form of **loans**. The interest rate applied by the SNB, known as the **'base rate'**, directly influences interest rates in Switzerland.

  For example, when the base rate rises, mortgage interest rates rise too.

- A high interest rate slows growth, because it becomes less attractive to borrow. On the other hand, high interest rates lower inflation.

- Low interest rates encourage investment, but create the risk of inflation.

  In January 2015, the SNB began applying negative interest rates in order to make the Swiss franc less attractive.

The **LIBOR** (London Interbank Offered Rate) is a reference rate for money markets. It is the rate at which banks lend to one another. In 2011, a scandal revealed that several banks, including UBS, had been colluding for several years to manipulate LIBOR. In 2012, UBS was fined 1.4 billion dollars by the US, British and Swiss authorities for these activities. LIBOR is expected to be phased out in 2021.

Types of activity

- There are three main types of banking activity:
  - **retail banking**, offering the 'classical' services for companies and individuals;
  - **wealth management**, providing services to wealthy clients (private banking) and investment management;
  - **investment banking**, comprising company financing and advisory services, as well as trading on the bank's own account (speculation with the money held by the bank).

  For example: raising money on capital markets, mergers and acquisitions, development of new financial instruments

Banks

Switzerland is one of the most important financial centres in the world. Its legendary banking secrecy has been under fire for the last few years.

The Swiss financial centre has given rise to many myths. Swiss banks are frequently featured in Hollywood thrillers, such as *The Bourne Identity, The Da Vinci Code, Munich, Inside Man* and the James Bond film *Casino Royale*.

The Swiss financial centre

- Approximately 6944 billion francs are managed by Swiss banks.

  Most of the big banks and commercial banks are headquartered in Zurich; private banks and wealth management companies are mainly in Geneva.

- Switzerland has 9% of the world market for **wealth management** (private and institutional) and holds third place after the USA (40%) and the UK (11%).

  Institutional wealth management relates essentially to pension funds.

- Swiss banks are renowned primarily for **private wealth management** (private banking) and hold first place in the world. Private banks have a special structure for this activity.

  Recently, several private banks have become limited companies (Pictet and Lombard Odier, for example).

Offshore private wealth management

USD billion

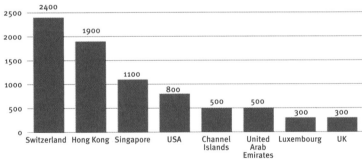

	USD billion
Switzerland	2400
Hong Kong	1900
Singapore	1100
USA	800
Channel Islands	500
United Arab Emirates	500
Luxembourg	300
UK	300

HOLLYWOOD IS GOING TO MAKE A FILM ABOUT BANKING SECRECY...

... A SILENT FILM!

Banking secrecy

- Banking secrecy has been based on federal law since 1934; Swiss banks are prohibited from disclosing information about their clients and the value of their deposits.

  This secrecy is not absolute: it can be countermanded by a judge in the context of a criminal prosecution, especially for money-laundering.

- Switzerland treats **tax fraud** (falsified salary records and accounts) as a penal offence, but not **tax evasion** (incomplete tax declaration). Tax evasion is subject only to administrative sanctions.

- This distinction is unique in the world and allowed Swiss banks to use banking secrecy to attract **non-declared funds from abroad** (····> p. 31).

Foreign pressure

- As a result of the 2007–2008 financial crisis, countries seeking to combat tax evasion (particularly the USA, France and Germany) forced Switzerland to apply the **standards laid down by the OECD** (Organisation for European Co-operation and Development) for mutual assistance in tax affairs. In 2009, the Federal Council abandoned the distinction between tax fraud and tax evasion for foreign clients.

  Switzerland was obliged to renegotiate several tax agreements with other countries. They may now request information on grounds of suspicion of tax evasion. This was not previously possible.

- Several scandals involving Swiss banks in the USA broke following the 2007–2008 crisis. **American prosecutors** opened proceedings against a dozen institutions accused of having abetted tax evasion.

  UBS settled for a fine of 780 million dollars and disclosure of data on its clients (see text on the right). The Wegelin bank's difficulties with the US courts forced it to close its operations after a fine of 58 million dollars.

- Switzerland now implements a system for automatic exchange of fiscal information between countries.

  European citizens can no longer easily conceal tax evasion behind Swiss banking secrecy. On the other hand, Swiss citizens who do not declare all their income or fortune benefit from bank secrecy as before.

The 'UBS affair' is often considered as ending bank secrecy. In 2009, UBS risked losing its banking licence in the USA because it had helped its clients cheat the US tax authorities. To save the bank, the Federal Council authorised the release of data on several thousand UBS clients. In 2012, Bradley Birkenfeld, a former employee, who had reported the bank to the US authorities, received a whistleblower reward of 104 million dollars after spending two years in prison.

THIS IS CALLED LIVING SAFELY IN SWITZERLAND!

Stock markets

Stock markets enable trade in raw materials (cocoa, coffee, etc.), currencies (dollars, euros, etc.) and securities (shares, bonds, etc.).

How stock markets work

• The best-known function of a stock market is for **trade in securities** (shares, bonds, etc.).

• When a company wants to be quoted on the stock market, it makes a public offering of its **shares** (⋯> p. 72). These shares can be resold at a price that changes constantly on the basis of the estimated value of the company.

Crises and Crashes

• When the stock market valuation of companies is vastly in excess of their real value, this is known as a **speculative bubble**. One occurred at the end of the 1990s as a result of the euphoria about new internet companies ('dotcom'). When the bubble burst in spring 2000, panic spread and all investors dumped their shares at the same time, leading to a massive fall in share prices.

• The 20th century has experienced several stock market crises. The worst was the **1929** crash on Wall Street (New York).

In October 1987, there was also a crash on the New York market; the Dow Jones index fell by 26.6% in a single day.

• In **2008,** the value of the largest companies quoted on the New York Stock Exchange plunged 34% because of the financial crisis.

This fall happened over several months, not on a single day; technically, it was not a crash.

At about 2.45 p.m. New York time on 6 May 2010, The Dow Jones index suddenly dropped by 9%, followed by an equally spectacular rise, all within a few minutes. This 'flash crash' drew attention to **high-frequency trading,** an automated transaction that uses computer algorithms. During several milliseconds, quicker than batting an eyelid, a very high volume of buy and sell orders were carried out in the hope of profits. In the USA, more than half of share transactions are carried out through high-frequency trading.

The Swiss stock market

In Switzerland, the stock market is called the **SIX Swiss Exchange**; it is an exclusively electronic trading platform. By value of securities quoted, the SIX is ranked 13th in the world (New York Stock Exchange 1, Nasdaq 2, Tokyo 3, London 4, Shanghai 5).

Stock market indices

The **SMI** (Swiss Market Index) is the main stock market index in Switzerland. It reflects the **performance** of some 20 large Swiss companies, such as Novartis, Nestlé, UBS and Swatch. Similar indices exist in all world financial centres, for example: the **Dow Jones** in New York; the **CAC 40** in Paris and the **Nikkei** in Tokyo.

Other indices track the movements of all quoted shares: In Switzerland, this index is called the SPI (Swiss Performance Index).

Insider trading is a crime that consists of using information that has not yet been published in order to undertake stock transactions. The former managers of Enron, who knew that their company was about to go under, sold their shares for several million dollars just before the spectacular bankruptcy of the company in 2001.

Stock market forecasts

The exact value and the future potential of companies are subject to many kinds of speculation. Investors use several methods to forecast the evolution of a stock. The two main ones are:
– **technical analysis**, that uses statistics to analyse market trends;
– **fundamental analysis**, that attempts to assess the real value of a company, using its balance sheet and accounts.

Financial products

There are many financial products, but all have in common that they can be bought and sold, generally on stock markets.

i HAD A GOLDEN YEAR ON THE STOCK MARKET!

Credit rating agencies give ratings to companies or public entities in relation to their capacity to reimburse. They have been strongly criticised for having given the highest rating (AAA or triple A) to financial products that packaged *subprime* loans; these products caused the 2007–2008 financial crisis (····> p. 74). Two agencies, Moody's and Standard & Poors, share 80% of the world market for credit rating.

Securities

Companies, banks and the State issue securities to raise capital and **finance** their activities. Purchase of securities is an **investment.**

Shares

- A share is part of the **capital** of a limited company.

- Buying shares entails a risk: if the company in question makes a profit, the shareholder will participate in the profits (**dividend**); if it goes bankrupt, the shareholder may lose all of the amount invested.

- The value of shares fluctuates according to the **financial health** of the company and its capacity to generate **future profits**.

- If shareholders sell their shares at a price higher than the purchase price, they make a **capital gain**.

Bonds

- A bond is part of a **loan** raised by the State, a big company (public or private) or a bank.

- Bondholders take **less risk** than shareholders, because the money advanced will be paid back at a given date and earns a rate of interest fixed in advance. Bondholders receive no dividends.

If the company goes bankrupt, bondholders may lose their money but are paid out before shareholders.

Derivatives

- A derivative is a **contract** between a seller and a purchaser for an operation (purchase or sale) for a **date, price** and **quantity** fixed in advance.

- The value of a derivative depends on the prospective value of the security (share or bond) on which it is based. The purchaser is **betting** on the **future value of the security**.

Funds

Funds are **portfolios** comprising several financial products (currencies, bonds, shares, derivatives). The **volume** of a fund can vary between several hundred million to several billion francs.

Investment funds

- Investment funds comprise a great variety of financial instruments.

- Investors buy one or several **units** of a fund. The price fluctuates according to the performance of the products that make up the fund.

- Funds are **diversified**; if the price of one of the shares in the fund falls, the price of the fund does not go down in the same proportion.

  Investment funds make it possible to invest in the stock market without mastering the intricacies of various financial instruments.

The vast majority of Swiss investors are in the stock market, often without being aware of it: part of the State pension scheme (AVS) is invested in financial markets; the same is true of company pension funds.

Hedge funds

- Hedge funds are created with a view to generating big profits mainly through **speculation**. They often comprise derivative products and aim to achieve results that do not depend on stock market trends.

- Their management requires a high degree of financial expertise. They are not for small investors.

Pension funds

- Pension funds are linked to one or more companies or institutions and finance the pensions of their **retired employees**.

- They are funded jointly by employees and employers.

- There are many in the USA, where there they finance the retirement of millions of people. In this capacity, they manage huge sums of money and are major participants in financial markets.

  Some 60% of US shares are held by pension funds; and these funds recognise no frontiers – more than a third of shares of companies quoted on the Paris stock exchange are held by pension funds in English-speaking countries.

The 2007–2008 financial crisis

The 'financial crisis' was actually a series of events: the US real estate crisis (from 2006), the banking crisis (from 2007), the world economic crisis (from 2009) and the debt crisis (from 2010).

The unprecedented impact of the US real estate crisis was caused by the **'packaging'** of mortgage debt to create financial instruments available to investors throughout the world. Investment banks used 'packaging' to put together extremely complex financial products that even succeeded in convincing the credit rating agencies (⸺> p. 72) to grant them AAA status, despite the fact that they were made up of highly risky loans.

The US real estate crisis

• Between 2002 and 2006, US real estate prices rose very quickly.

• Caught up in the euphoria of a market in full growth mode, US banks offered more and more mortgage loans to people with limited ability to reimburse. These poor-quality loans were known as **'subprime'**.

• From 2006, house prices fell everywhere in the USA. The **real estate bubble** had burst.

When market participants no longer believe that prices will continue to rise, they stop bidding and prices return very rapidly to a 'normal' level. A real estate bubble only becomes visible when it bursts. The fact that prices collapsed all at once shows that the rise of previous years was speculative.

US trends in real estate prices

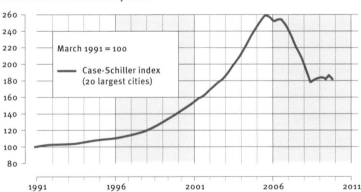

March 1991 = 100

Case-Schiller index (20 largest cities)

Three factors contributed to the US housing bubble:
- the US central bank, fearing deflation after the dotcom bubble and the 9/11 attacks, held **interest rates very low** between 2002 and 2006, encouraging people to take on debt;
- large **amounts of foreign capital** came into the USA, increasing demand for profitable investments;
- the poor quality of subprime mortgages was hidden by the **extreme complexity of the instruments**, and few people understood the risks (see opposite).

The world banking crisis

- From the summer of 2007, many banks realised that they had invested in poor quality loans, by holding financial instruments backed by risky mortgages (**asset-backed securities – ABS**). The price of these products collapsed.

  Subprime asset-backed securities lost 70% of their value in a single year, between autumn 2007 and autumn 2008.

- Some banks found that their losses were so high that they could no longer honour their debts and were close to bankruptcy.

  By definition, a bank is always more indebted than a normal company. If clients fear bank insolvency, a panic may lead them to withdraw their deposits all at once. The bank no longer has any liquidity and goes immediately into bankruptcy.

- Confidence between banks disappears and they are no longer willing to provide credit to one another. This is a very dangerous situation, because if there are no interbank loans, the economy is paralysed.

- To avoid this danger, the main central banks provided banks with very large short-term loans and saved some from bankruptcy. The situation seemed under control for over a year.

- Then, on 15 September 2008, Lehmann Brothers, a US investment bank, declared bankruptcy. To general surprise, the US government did not step in to rescue the bank.

- Lehmann Brothers' bankruptcy was a massive shock. From one day to the next, the crisis had become global. Throughout the world, **central banks and governments intervened** to rescue their banks

  In Switzerland, UBS was rescued after Lehmann Brothers' bankruptcy. This State intervention provoked a heated debate about the problem of big banks (⋯⋯⟩ p. 91).

If it hasn't rained for a long time, more and more people go out without an umbrella, because the chances of being surprised by a shower seem negligible. In the field of economics, humans behave in the same way: when there has been a long period of uninterrupted growth, they take more risks in the financial market. During the two decades before the 2007–2008 crisis, inflation was under control. The age of major economic fluctuations seemed over. Even the bursting of the dotcom bubble and the terrorist attacks of 9/11 had not provoked a major economic crisis. This excessive confidence explains why banks did not foresee the subprime crisis.

DON'T JUMP OUT OF THE WINDOW...

...IT MIGHT CREATE A PANIC!

The 2007–2008 financial crisis

The effects of the financial crisis are still being felt today, with an unprecedented debt crisis, particularly in the USA and Europe.

The world economic crisis

- At the end of 2008, the effects of the financial crisis were apparent in all sectors of the economy. **Share prices** fell heavily, and there was a major decline in international trade.

  Between September 2008 and March 2009, the SMI index of the Swiss stock exchange lost 40% of its value. Within a few months, international trade flows declined by an unprecedented 30%.

- In 2009, the economic situation worsened throughout the world.

  For many countries, it was the worst economic crisis since the Great Depression of the 1930s (not counting World War II).

- Western countries adopted two main measures to attempt to limit the effects of the crisis:
  - in order to stimulate demand, governments made massive increases in **state spending**; some called it a return to **Keynesian** economic policies (⤑ p. 22);
  - central banks adopted an even more highly expansive monetary policy, lowering interest rates and increasing the **money supply** (⤑ p. 64).

- From 2010, the US and the main European economies began to grow again.

The European debt crisis

- Due to the recession and chronic state budgetary deficits, **public debt** increased in several European countries.

  The English acronym PIGS (Portugal, Ireland, Greece, Spain) is a derogatory term widely used to indicate the worst offenders of budgetary rigour. Italy is sometimes also mentioned in this category (PIIGS).

- A **vicious circle** was created: the more a country is indebted, the greater the risk of default and the higher the interest rates necessary to service the debt (poor risks incur higher costs).

  Government bonds in these countries, hitherto considered as safe investments, were suddenly subject to speculative pressure from investors, fearing that the bonds would never be honoured.

- In the spring of 2010, **European banks** faced another crisis: several of them had lent to over-indebted countries in the eurozone. Once again, as during the worst moments of the subprime crisis, the health of their balance sheets was threatened,

  The classical solution to this kind of problem is a reduction ('restructuring') of debt. Normally, creditors recognise that they have been imprudent in granting too many loans and agree to bear part of this restructuring cost. However, the European banks were already under-capitalised as a result of the financial crisis and governments refused this option.

- After a first rescue package for Greece, the eurozone governments set up in May 2010 a **European Financial Stability Facility** (replaced in 2011 by the **European Stability Mechanism**), in order to assist countries experiencing similar problems in the future.

- In 2011, an agreement was reached, under which private banks cancelled about half the debts owed them by Greece. Greece accepted, as a counterpart, to make budget cuts.

  Several other countries (Spain, Portugal, Italy and France) continue to suffer from debt problems.

Goldman Sachs, the US investment bank, is known to have made much money from the collapse of the subprime market. It also played a key role in the Greek debt crisis, helping the Greek government hide the worrying state of its public finances. This controversial company has employed many politicians who have gone on to high government positions. These include the former President of the European Central Bank, Mario Draghi; the former Italian Prime Minister, Mario Monti; and the former US Treasury Secretary, Hank Paulson.

...and in the USA

- The US national (federal) debt reached approximately **25,000 billion dollars,** more than 100% of GDP (against only 59% in 2002).

- The US Congress regularly fixes **debt ceilings** to slow expansion of the debt, without much success.

  The US debt situation is just as serious as that of the eurozone – but since financial markets never doubt the credit repayment ability of the US government, the consequences are less dramatic.

FOR MY DEBTS
TO YOU.
THANKS

Foreign trade

The globalisation of the economy
The WTO
Switzerland and Europe
North–South relations

The globalisation of the economy

Globalisation is a vast process of liberalisation of trade in goods, services and capital throughout the world. It is linked to the development of competition and technological innovation, particularly in transport and communications.

Change of work sites is not a new phenomenon. In the 19th century, moves were made to rural areas, where wages were lower and trade unions weak or badly organised.

History

- The foundation of globalisation goes back to the **Age of Discovery** (15th to 17th century). At this time the first international companies were formed.

  For example, the Dutch East India Company was one of the first shareholding companies.

- The **Industrial Revolution** (19th century) gave rise to a considerable increase in productivity and forced companies to look for new markets for their products. Large industrial groups were formed (Nestlé in Switzerland, Siemens in Germany, Ericsson in Sweden). Trade increased exponentially up to World War I.

- The two world wars put a stop to globalisation and there was no major growth in international trade until **the 1960s**.

- A major movement for the liberalisation of trade was initiated by the developed countries with the creation of the General Agreement on Tariffs and Trade (GATT) in 1947 (····} p. 82), succeeded by the World Trade Organisation (WTO) in 1995.

- The collapse of the Soviet Union in **the early 1990s** pushed globalisation forward, opening new markets in the international economy.

  Liberal economic policies triumphed almost everywhere on the planet, even – to a certain extent – in communist China.

  - Many **factors** gave rise to **globalisation**:
    - the lowering of customs tariffs (from 40% to 5% on average), stimulating a growth in trade;
    - freeing of **capital movements,** allowing companies to invest easily abroad and benefit from low labour costs;
    - fall in the **cost of air transport**;
    - development of **telecommunications**;
    - creation of vast **free trade areas** (EU, Mercosur, ALENA, ASEAN);
    - increase in the number of member States of the **WTO** (····} p. 82).

Unintended effects

- Competition from lower wages in certain countries tends to **push down the wages** of unskilled workers in developed countries and contribute to **unemployment**.

- International speculation occurs. Some investors have a **short-term view** and seek immediate profits. This weakens the economy of some regions.

- Ultra-rapid industrialisation in some parts of the world (e.g. China) takes no account of collateral damage (**pollution, exploitation** of some parts of the population, over-exploitation of natural resources).

- The decisions taken by the main participants in globalisation (G7, WTO, IMF, World Bank) exclude many poor countries from the process. This widens the **North–South divide** (···▶ p. 83).

> GLOBALISATION IS TAKING GIGANTIC STEPS FORWARD!

Opportunities

- **World division of labour** is increasing, in accordance with the theory of comparative advantage (···▶ p. 7). Increases in global wealth should follow and, in time, disparities should diminish.

- To be able to participate fully in world trade, poorer countries must develop their infrastructure and implement certain health and safety standards.

- **The G20**, which brings together the 20 main economies of the world, was set up in 1999 to take account of the interests of emerging nations in international discussions. Since the 2007–2008 financial crisis, it has gained considerably in importance.

Switzerland has not been invited to join the G20.

The unintended effects of globalisation have led to the creation of several 'anti-globalisation' movements, among which two of the best organised are *Attac* and the *World Social Forum*. For most of them, globalisation is a given, but they ask that certain measures be implemented to limit collateral damage, especially more regulation by governments.

The WTO

The World Trade Organization (WTO) is responsible for rules governing international trade. It regulates trade in a multilateral context (between several partners).

The WTO set up a dispute settlement system that allows member States to resolve conflicts in cases of violation of WTO agreements. In 2019, the administration of US President Donald Trump blocked the WTO procedure for settlement of disputes, a mechanism of special importance for small countries like Switzerland since it protects them against unilateral policies of the large countries.

From GATT to WTO

- In the aftermath of World War II, the development of international trade was seen as an absolute priority by the Western powers. In 1947, 23 developed countries set up the General Agreement on Tariffs and Trade (**GATT**) with a view to reducing progressively their customs tariffs and other obstacles to trade. Switzerland became a member in 1966.

- The GATT was the forum for a successive series of negotiations (known as 'rounds'). In the 1960s, rapid development of trade within Europe led directly to the '**Kennedy Round**' negotiations. This 'round', from 1964–1967, made major progress in reducing customs tariffs and non-tariff barriers to trade. The subsequent '**Tokyo Round**' (1975–1979) started the extension of trade liberalisation to the third world.

- The '**Uruguay Round**' began in 1986. Its aims were ambitious, envisaging an expansion of GATT coverage to important new areas such as services, capital, intellectual property, textiles, and agriculture. 123 countries took part in the round. It was the first time developing countries had played an active role in international trade negotiations.

The ambitious goals of the Uruguay Round were only partly achieved. Two new agreements on agriculture and on subsidies and countervailing measures were signed, but many details were left to subsequent negotiations. On services, a similar result was achieved by the adoption of the GATS Agreement (the General Agreement on Trade in Services).

- The creation of the WTO led to a series of **conferences** with the objective of maintaining momentum in freeing trade.

In 1999, at the Seattle conference, developing countries ("the South") opposed trade liberalisation that was too much slanted in favour of the developed countries ("the North"). The conference was a failure and ended with no new agreement.

- The **Doha Round**, launched in 2001 at a ministerial conference in Qatar, made much slower progress than hoped and no agreement has yet been reached.

The North–South divide

- The WTO is at the heart of a conflict between developed and developing countries ('North–South').

- Rich countries demand the opening of 'southern' markets to their goods and services but maintain barriers that prevent the developing countries from exporting their **agricultural products**.

- Some **protest groups** view the WTO as an instrument at the service of the developed world.

- Others consider that freeing international trade gives developing countries opportunities to increase income through exports.

Switzerland and the WTO

- The Federal Council aims to pursue the liberalisation of trade with its partners.

- Now that the WTO negotiations are at a standstill, countries are looking at bilateral (two-country) co-operation.

- At the centre of these discussions there is the hot topic of **agriculture**, which remains highly protected in Switzerland; major reforms will be necessary before trade liberalisation can continue in this sector.

Exports of goods and services
(billion dollars 2018)

1. China	2487
2. USA	1664
3. Germany	1561
20. Switzerland	311

Imports of goods and services
(billion dollars 2018)

1. USA	2614
2. China	2136
3. Germany	1286
18. Switzerland	279

Switzerland and Europe

The European Union is Switzerland's main economic partner. Switzerland is not a member of the EU but is profoundly affected by the decisions taken in Brussels, especially in the economic sphere.

If the EU were a country, it would, with its 446 million inhabitants, be the third most populous country in the world (after China and India). It would contribute approximately one fifth of world GDP. Switzerland, with 8 million inhabitants, contributes a little less than 1% of world GDP.

The European Union (EU)

- The EU comprises **27 member States**. It resembles a confederation of States, similar in some respects to Switzerland in its early stages.

- The EU's objective is to **integrate** the various European economies in a vast **common market**, so as to avoid all risks of a return to war.

- Today, this common market has been realised and 19 States have even adopted a common currency, the **euro**, that has been in circulation since **2002**.

- Three key dates in the development of the EU:
  - 1957: the **Treaty of Rome**. creating the European Economic Community (EEC);
  - 1986: the **Single European Act**, which provided for free circulation of persons, services and capital;
  - 1992: the **Maastricht Treaty**, which marked the start of the European economic and monetary union.

The European Free Trade Association (EFTA)

EFTA was set up in 1960 and created a **free trade area** between the States that did not join the European Union. Once comprising nine members, it only has four today (the others having joined the EU): Iceland, Liechtenstein, Norway and Switzerland.

The European Economic Area (EEA)

With the exception of Switzerland, all the other EFTA members are also members of the EEA, together with the EU members. The EEA provides for the **free movement** of goods, services, capital and persons between its members.

The agreements between Switzerland and the EU

- The **1972 free trade agreement** between Switzerland and the EU created a free trade area by the **elimination of customs tariffs** for industrial products.

- After 1992, when Swiss voters refused entry into the European Economic Area, Switzerland signed a number of **bilateral agreements** with the EU, strengthening economic ties between the two parties, in areas such as **agriculture**, **transport**, **research** and **technical barriers to trade**. From 2002, these agreements also cover free **movement of persons**.

A special relationship

- In 2019, Switzerland exported more than 312 billion francs' worth of goods; 50% went to the EU.

  Germany, alone, represents 15% of Swiss exports of goods; the USA 14%.

- In 2019, Switzerland's imports of goods totalled 276.1 billion francs; 59% came from the EU.

  More than 20% of the total came from Germany.

In 1979, Germany prohibited importation of the French blackcurrant liqueur **Cassis de Dijon**, on the grounds that its alcohol content was below the legal minimum in Germany. The European Court of Justice decided against Germany on the ground that it had restrained trade in goods. As a result, a product that is legal in one EU member State is now also legal in all the others, unless it is against the public interest. Since 2010, Switzerland applies the same principle in trade with the EU.

The future of Swiss-EU relations

- **Tax harmonisation** is an important topic of negotiation. The EU accuses Switzerland of providing hidden subsidies to certain companies by giving them tax advantages (⤑ p. 31).

- Voters' acceptance of an anti-immigration initiative on 9 February 2014 led to a worsening of Swiss–EU relations.

- On 27 September 2020, the Swiss people massively rejected a measure that would have ended free movement of persons between Switzerland and the EU.

North–South Relations

Development in poorer countries is one of the major challenges of the world economy. It is also one of the priorities of Swiss foreign policy.

Developing countries

- During the **industrial revolution** of the 19th century, Europe and North America experienced tremendous development. The economies of their colonies, situated in the southern hemisphere, remained mainly **agricultural**.

- Toward the middle of the 20th century, **decolonisation** allowed several countries in the South to gain independence. But their economies had problems adapting.

- Developed countries had loaned large sums of money to the countries of the South with a view to allowing them to develop their economies. However, the **debt crisis** of the early 1980s showed that many developing countries were unable to pay back these loans.

- Today, the divide between rich and poor countries is enormous. Almost half the world's population lives on less than two dollars a day.

The 2018 GDP per capita of Switzerland was 80,721 francs. That of Burundi, one of the poorest countries, was 260 francs.

The IMF and the World Bank

- The International Monetary Fund (**IMF**) was set up in 1944 to guarantee the stability of the international monetary system. In the mid 1970s, the IMF changed direction by providing loans to countries with economic difficulties. The IMF loans were conditional on the adoption by the beneficiaries of liberal economic policies, opening their markets and privatising public companies.

- The World Bank was set up in 1945 to finance reconstruction after World War II. Just like the IMF, the World Bank has subsequently concentrated primarily on developing countries. It also supports many projects aimed at poverty reduction.

Development Aid

- The developed countries are active in the developing world through **aid programmes**. Their aim is to promote growth and maintain peace, but also to advance their own **geopolitical objectives**.

  During the Cold War, the USA provided massive assistance to African countries in the form of 'development aid' with the aim of creating a bulwark against communism.

- In Switzerland, development aid is managed by the **SDC** (Swiss Agency for Development and Cooperation). This agency supports and implements projects for **poverty reduction**, **security**, **human rights**, **democracy** and the **rule of law**. It also provides emergency **humanitarian aid** in situations of catastrophe and conflict abroad.

Public development aid 2019
(% of GDP)

Luxembourg	1.02
Norway	1.02
Sweden	0.99
Denmark	0.71
Switzerland	0.44
France	0.44
USA	0.16

Trade with developing countries

- In addition to the aid provided by the SDC, Switzerland contributes, through the State Secretariat for Economic Affairs (**SECO**), towards **economic development,** with the aim of helping a certain number of countries to make the transition to a market economy; this is intended to enable them to **integrate** into the world economy and also to promote Swiss exports.

- Switzerland also seeks to develop bilateral economic relations with developing countries.

  For example, free trade agreements with Morocco, Lebanon, Chile, Mexico and Tunisia

Challenges for the Swiss economy

Changes in banking practice
The open economy
Disparities
The economy and the environment

Changes in banking practice

The 2007–2008 financial crisis had two main consequences for the Swiss financial centre: it reinforced international pressure against Swiss banking secrecy and it revealed the systemic economic risks that the banks can create.

Do Swiss banks have the means to implement the 'clean money' strategy? It is now very difficult for US and European citizens to evade taxes on funds held in Switzerland. Some 20 other countries have also concluded agreements with Switzerland for the automatic exchange of tax information on request, in accordance with OECD standards (····> p. 69). Citizens of other countries, however, can still deposit non-declared funds in Switzerland.

A 'clean money' strategy

Under international pressure (····> p. 69), the Swiss government announced in 2012 a 'clean money' strategy. It marked the start of a new era for Swiss banks, that had to abandon a business model based on the management of non-declared funds.

The relevant legislation still refers to banking secrecy, but does not guarantee confidentiality for foreigners depositing non-declared funds in Switzerland.

Pressure from European countries

- The EU insisted that Switzerland accept the **automatic exchange** of tax information and follow European standards.

- In order to avoid this constraint, Switzerland proposed a withholding tax at source (known as 'Rubik'), that was intended to allow European clients to pay their taxes while retaining anonymity. European pressure led to the abandonment of this proposal, and Switzerland now accepts the principle of automatic exchange of information.

Pressure from the USA

- In negotiations with the US legal authorities, and with the approval of the Federal Council, Swiss banks **handed over data** on their clients and employees.

- In addition, Switzerland collaborates with the USA in the implementation of the new Foreign Account Tax Compliance Act (**FATCA**) that requires the disclosure of data on the accounts of all US citizens living abroad.

Several Swiss banks severed relations with all their clients resident in the USA, in order to avoid any conflict with American law.

The 'Big Bank' problem

- The 2007–2008 financial crisis was caused by the high level of risk taken by the banks, particularly those of **'systemic' importance** (essential to the proper functioning of the whole financial system).

- These banks are considered 'too big to fail' since their failure would endanger the whole economy of a country.

  In Switzerland, UBS, Credit Suisse, Raiffeisen, Postfinance and the Zurich cantonal bank fall in this category.

- These banks enjoy an **implicit guarantee from the State**, because they know that, in the last resort, they will be protected from collapse. This encourages them to take unreasonable risks, by, for example taking excessive debt or making loans at lower interest rates than their competitors.

- A new Swiss law correcting this situation came into force in 2012. Its most important measure is the requirement for banks to increase the level of their own equity ('own funds'), thereby reducing the risk that the State would have to step in to rescue them.

Just before the 2007–2008 financial crisis, UBS's own funds represented only 2% of its total assets. This meant that the bank was financed almost entirely from sources other than those of the bank's owners! On 16 October 2008, at the height of the crisis, UBS was rescued by the Swiss Confederation, because the failure of this giant (25,000 employees, 70,000 companies receiving finance, 20% of the country's savings) would have been a disaster for the entire Swiss economic system.

High risk activities

- The nature of **investment banking** leads the big banks to take inordinate risks. Some economists recommend that big banks should be **divided up** into smaller corporate entities; this would allow failure without compromising the whole economic system.

- In the USA, the Dodd-Frank law for reform of Wall Street limits the activities of banks in **trading for their own account** (⋯⟩ p. 67).

  Traders in big banks can very quickly lose large sums of money. In 2011, a trader at UBS lost 2 billion francs of the bank's money through unauthorised transactions.

The open economy

For the Swiss economy, future growth opportunities will come primarily from outside the country; new markets must be found for growth in exports of goods and services. At the same time, the arrival of foreign competition on the Swiss market ought to stimulate Swiss companies to be both innovative and competitive.

International trade

- During the 20th century, most countries experienced a huge growth in their **imports** and **exports**. This trend was reinforced by the shift in the economies of Eastern Europe towards a market system in the 1990s.

*When a country exports more than it imports, it runs a **trade surplus**. This is the case for Switzerland, Germany and China. On the other hand, the USA, India and Serbia run a **trade deficit**.*

- Trade policy fluctuates between two main tendencies:
  - **protectionism**: the State prevents foreign companies from competing against local companies, for example, by putting up **tariff or other barriers**;
  - **openness**: the State reaches **free trade** agreements to enable exporters to gain access to new markets. As a counterpart, it opens its own frontiers to the products of foreign companies.

Switzerland's main exports in 2019 (billion francs)

SWITZERLAND NEEDS MANY HELPING HANDS.

TO WEAR ITS WATCHES!

Exports of Swiss watches rose from 10.3 billion francs in 2000 to 21.7 billion in 2019.

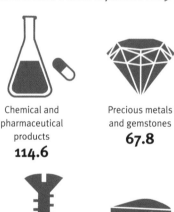

Chemical and pharmaceutical products
114.6

Precious metals and gemstones
67.8

Watch-making and jewellery
33.4

Machinery and electronics
32.1

Metals and tools
30.6

Food, beverages and tobacco
9.1

Vehicles
5.7

Energy
2.5

Reciprocal advantages

- Free trade brings new **opportunities** for companies. Switzerland's foreign economic policy aims to facilitate their access to new markets by:

  - multilateral (multi-state) negotiations in the WTO;

  - bilateral agreements with States or groups of States;

  - support for Swiss exporters.

- When frontiers are open to **foreign competition,** the market becomes more **competitive**. This offers several advantages for the Swiss economy:

  - stimulation of **innovation;**

    Swiss companies must differentiate themselves from their competitors.

  - **higher productivity**.

    By opening its frontiers to the EU, Switzerland benefits from a young and qualified work force that supports growth.

Switzerland is late

- By staying outside the movement for **European integration,** Switzerland has delayed opening its markets to the world.

  For example, it was only due to pressure from the EU that Switzerland liberalised its electricity market.

- Some **lobbies** (pressure groups) have a great influence on the Federal Assembly and oppose liberalisation projects that threaten their economic interests.

  For example, the pharmaceutical industry and agriculture.

Disparities

The growth of the world economy since the end of World War II has considerably reduced poverty in developed countries; but disparities remain and have been increasing for a few years.

In Switzerland, the monthly salary of a salesperson in a supermarket is less than 4000 francs. This is the approximate equivalent of the amount earned by the head of the Novartis company in 45 minutes (salary of 10.6 million francs in 2019).

Origins

Income disparities within the population are linked to one or several factors:
– social or family origin;
– education;
– the economic sector in which employment is found;
– degree of experience and seniority in the company;
– age and gender.

The poverty threshold

- The definition of the poverty threshold is subject to debate. The lower it is fixed, the fewer people are considered as poor and the lower is the amount of State financial assistance for this group.

- The Swiss Conference for Social Assistance ('Conférence Suisse des institutions d'action sociale') has fixed the poverty threshold at 2293 francs per month for a single person. This amount is estimated to cover basic needs, rent and health costs.

The 'working poor'

- A person who works but is unable to earn enough to stay out of poverty is part of the 'working poor'.

  - In Switzerland, some 8% of the active population belongs to this category.

  - Single-parent households and couples with more than three children are at greater risk of becoming part of the working poor. Women and foreigners are disproportionately represented compared with the rest of the population.

State intervention

- In order to diminish disparities, the Swiss government has adopted a series of **social benefit programmes**. Some of these allow the poorest segment of the population to achieve a minimum standard of living.

- **Social assistance** is distributed by the cantons. It is paid out as a last resort to ensure the survival of its beneficiaries, in particular when they have exhausted their rights to unemployment and reintegration benefits.

- The biggest component of State social spending is for **retirement** pensions (AVS).

  The monthly AVS pension of a single person is 1185 francs and the maximum 2370 francs. In addition, 17% of retired persons receive additional benefits due to their precarious financial situation.

Challenges for the Swiss economy

If the number of poor people in Switzerland has sharply diminished in the last fifty years, there are still a number of factors creating hardship:

- As in all European countries, the increase in life expectancy creates a problem for the **financing of pensions**.

  A minimum level of pension must be guaranteed in order to avoid condemning a whole segment of society to poverty, but the cost of these benefits continues to increase. Should contributions to the State pension scheme be increased? Should the retirement age be increased? Should pensions be reduced?

- Income disparities are increasing in Switzerland. They are more marked than in France and the Scandinavian countries, but less than in the USA and Italy.

- Switzerland also has an interest in the reduction of disparities beyond its frontiers and should aim, over time, to increase its trade with developing countries.

The economy and the environment

The development of the world economy since the 19th century industrial revolution has been accompanied by an increase in pollution. Awareness of this phenomenon is not recent, but has increased in urgency in the last few years.

Growth

- All economies want to grow. The vast majority of politicians favour growth.

- Economic growth is always accompanied by an increase in **negative effects on the environment**.

  The walls of London houses were black at the end of the 19th century, covered in soot from factory chimneys. This phenomenon was eliminated by diminishing the use of coal and decentralising factories, but it is still present in some cities in China and India.

- Growth goes hand in hand with the increase in consumption of goods and services, as well as in transport (particularly road and air), which increases **energy use** and **pollution**.

- Current growth trends in the world economy are a very real threat to the **environment**; the resources of the planet are not sufficient to satisfy continually increasing demand, and our ecosystem is unable to eliminate all the waste and gas emissions produced in the economy.

The concept of 'negative growth' rejects the objective of economic growth. The supporters of this movement consider that uncontrolled production is responsible for the exhaustion of natural resources and, as a result, the term 'sustainable development' (····> p. 99) is an intellectual fraud. With the acceleration of climate change, there are more and more supporters of negative growth.

POLLUTION ON MY WAY TO WORK... POLLUTION AT WORK... POLLUTION GOING HOME...

...i SHOULD HAVE STAYED iN BED!

The energy problem

Most of the energy consumed is non-renewable.

Non-renewable energies *(85% of world consumption)*

- **Oil** is highly polluting. Available resources could be exhausted in 50 to 100 years: 35% of world energy consumption.

- **Gas** is less polluting. Available resources could be exhausted in 150 to 200 years: 15% of world energy consumption.

- **Coal** is the most polluting form of energy: 25% of world energy consumption. Available resources are abundant.

- Nuclear power does not emit greenhouse gases but produces waste products that cannot be eliminated.

  According to a study by the Federal Office for Civil Defence, the explosion of a nuclear plant in Switzerland would cost the national economy more than 4000 billion francs (10 times annual GDP). In addition, a large part of the country would be uninhabitable for several centuries.

A poorly insulated apartment, heated at 23°C, equipped with traditional electric bulbs, in which the occupants take one bath a day and do not turn off electrical appliances that are not being used, consumes three times more energy than an apartment of identical size, heated at 19°C, and in which the occupants are careful with water and electricity.

Renewable energies *(15% of world consumption)*

- **Geothermal** (harnessing heat from underground) and **hydraulic** (from dams) energy are highly developed in some countries.

- **Solar and wind power** provide only a tiny proportion of world consumption (less than 1%) but are likely to grow substantially.

Energy in Switzerland

- Heat for buildings and water consumes 37% of energy consumed in Switzerland, 31% for transport, 29% for electrical appliances and 3% for lighting.

- **Petroleum products** provide 51% of energy consumed in Switzerland.

- **Electricity** represents 25% of energy consumption in Switzerland.

  Sixty percent of electricity is generated by hydraulic power (dams and rivers), 34% by nuclear power (five plants in Switzerland) and 2% by geothermal plants. One percent comes from solar and wind power.

The economy and the environment

In the last 30 years, the average surface temperature of the globe has increased by 0.6°C. It may also increase by several degrees during the 21st century, mainly due to human activity.

Methane represents about 20% of all greenhouse gas emissions. Some 40% of methane emissions come from the stomach gases of cows (one cow produces between 110 and 500 litres of methane a day). This problem is far from being solved: a UN report forecasts that world meat consumption will double by 2050.

Global warming

- The main cause of global warming is the increase in emissions of **greenhouse gases,** the main component of which is carbon dioxide (**CO$_2$**).

  CO$_2$ emissions have more than doubled since 1970.

- Other things are also accelerating the warming process:
  - the **melting of the glaciers and sea ice,** also due to global warming, diminishes the reflection of the sun's rays;
  - deforestation reduces the number of trees that transform CO$_2$ into oxygen;
  - the **vapour trail from planes** creates artificial clouds that block infrared rays escaping from earth into the atmosphere.

- Global warming causes **rises in the sea level, droughts, torrential rain** and violent **cyclones,** major **movements of people,** the diminution of **biodiversity** (disappearance of numerous animal species) and the **melting of the glaciers and sea ice**.

Evolution of CO$_2$ emissions
Projections of the US Energy Information Administration

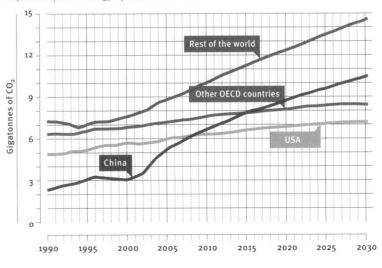

Sustainable development

Climate conferences

- At the Earth Summit in Rio de Janeiro in 1992, 179 States adopted Agenda 21, that included measures (environmental, social, economics and health) to guarantee the sustainable development of the planet in the 21st century.

- The 1997 **Kyoto Protocol** envisioned a reduction of approximately 5% in greenhouse gas emissions between 1990 and 2012.

  In the industrialised countries, this objective has been only partially achieved. During this period, CO_2 emissions have greatly increased in the developing countries, especially in China and India.

- In 2012, the **Doha Conference** on climate change attempted to extend the Kyoto Protocol until 2020, with limited success.

  Several large polluting countries, including the USA, China, Japan, Brazil and India, refused any binding commitments.

- In 2015, 195 countries signed the **Paris Agreement** with the objective of limiting global warming by 1.5°C and 2°C by 2100.

The concept of **sustainable development** was defined for the first time in 1987 by the former Norwegian Prime Minister Gro Brundtland, who chaired the World Commission on Environment and Development of the United Nations. Her report, *Our Common Future*, states: "Sustainable development is development that meets the needs of the present without compromising the ability of future generations to meet their own needs."

In Switzerland

- The **CO_2** law, revised in 2020, aims for a 50% reduction in the 1990 level of emissions.

  One of the measures in place is a tax on CO_2, levied on fossil fuel (heating oil, gas, coal).

- Thanks to technological progress, current energy consumption levels can be lowered and new and less polluting types of energy can be developed.

  More and more new building projects and renovations receive the "Minergie" label. It encourages economies in the use of energy (insulation and choice of materials) and use of renewable energy sources (solar, geothermal and long-distance heating).

Glossary

A

ALENA – Free trade area comprising the USA, Canada and Mexico.

Anticyclical – Describes a budgetary policy that aims to counteract the effects of economic cycles.

ASEAN – Association of Southeast Asian Nations, including a free trade area.

Assets – Total of what a company owns.

Autarchy – Economic system of a country that is self-sufficient and refuses trade with other countries.

AVS/AHV/OASI – Swiss State pension scheme.

B

Balance of payments – Accounting of all transactions between a given country and the outside world, including the balance of trade.

Balance of trade – Difference between the value of a country's imports and exports.

Balance sheet – Table showing assets and liabilities of a company at a given moment.

Banking secrecy – Principle founded in Swiss law that prohibits banks from revealing information on their clients.

Base lending rate – Interest rate determined by the national bank that influences the interest rates applied by banks.

Bilateral – Relationship between two States, for example freeing trade.

Board – Organ of a limited company appointed by the General Meeting to manage the company.

Bond – Negotiable financial instrument representing a loan to a company or public body.

Broker – Person who trades in financial products (also called 'trader').

Budget – Accounting forecasts of revenue and expenditure.

Budget deficit – Situation in which the expenses of a public entity during a given period are higher than its revenue.

C

Cantonal bank – Bank with one third or more capital and voting rights held by the canton.

Capital – All financial assets of a company.

Capitalism – Economic and social system in which the means of production are held privately.

Cartel – Understanding between several companies to limit competition in their sector.

Cassis de Dijon – Principle that allows all products legally produced in the EU to be automatically accepted in Switzerland.

Central bank – State monetary authority that issues banknotes and decides monetary policy.

Communism – Doctrine under which the State holds all means of production and ensures equitable distribution.

Company governance – Set of internal company rules determining transparency and relations between shareholders, management and board of directors.

Comparative advantage – Theory developed by David Ricardo, proving the usefulness of foreign trade.

Competition – Situation that encourages companies to offer optimal price and quality.

Crash – Sudden major collapse of stock market values.

Crisis – Turning point after a phase of economic expansion prior to a recession.

D

Deflation – A lengthy fall in the general price level (opposite of inflation).

Demand – Quantity of goods or services that purchasers are ready to buy at a given price.

Depression – Particularly long period of recession.

Derivative – Financial product based on a forecast of a future transaction at conditions fixed in advance.

Dividend – Participation in profit allocated to each share of a limited company.

Dow Jones – Main index of the New York stock exchange, reflecting the performance of some thirty US companies.

E

Economic cycle – Cycle comprising a period of economic growth, a halt and a downward phase.

Economiesuisse – Main trade association of Swiss companies.

EEA – European Economic Area, comprising all EU countries and EFTA countries, except Switzerland.

EFTA – European Free Trade Association, a free trade area comprising four non-member States of the EU (Iceland, Liechtenstein, Norway and Switzerland).

Expansion – Phase of economic growth.

F

Federal Department of Economic Affairs – One of the seven federal departments of the Swiss government.

Financial instrument – Negotiable document establishing a right, e.g. a share or bond.

Foreign currency – National money (franc, dollar, euro, etc.).

Free trade – Economic system promoting interstate trade.

G

G20 – Ministerial meeting comprising 20 countries (industrialised and emerging) considered more representative than G7.

G7 – Ministerial meeting comprising the seven main industrialised countries: Canada, France, Germany, Italy, Japan, United Kingdom and USA.

GATT – General Agreement on Tariffs and Trade set up in 1947, succeeded by WTO in 1995.

GDP – Gross Domestic Product, annual value of all produce in a given territory.

Globalisation – Process for freeing global trade.

Gross national income – Economic indicator similar to GDP, but including income from foreign residents but excluding income earned in the domestic economy by non-residents.

Growth – Increase in economic activity, normally measured by the year to year evolution of the GDP.

H

Hedge fund – Fund comprising mainly derivative products.

Holding company – Financial company holding shares in other companies.

I

IMF – International Monetary Fund – grants credits to countries with balance of payments problems.

Industrial revolution – In the 19th century, transition from a mainly agricultural society to an industrial society.

Inflation – Rise over time in the price level.

Insider trading – Crime resulting from a profit in share trading using information that has not yet been made public.

Interest rate – Rate of remuneration of capital.

Interventionism – Doctrine of State intervention in economic affairs.

Investment – Utilisation of capital for the purpose of increasing the production or profitability of a company.

Investment fund – Traditional fund comprising shares and bonds.

IPC – Swiss consumer price index showing the evolution in the cost of a basket of goods and services commonly purchased by households.

K

Keynesianism – Economic theory based on the work of John Maynard Keynes that argues for interventionism and an anti-cyclical budgetary policy.

Kyoto Protocol

Kyoto Protocol – Treaty negotiated in 1997 in the Japanese town of Kyoto – the 162 signatory States undertook to reduce their emission of greenhouse gases.

L

Liabilities – Total of what a company owes its creditors and owners.

Liberalisation – Process consisting in the reduction of State intervention in the economy.

Liberalism – Economic doctrine arguing that the State should refrain from interfering with the free play of competition.

Libor – London interbank offered rate, an average of the interest rates offered by several banks, used as a reference in money markets.

Limited company – Company owned by shareholders whose personal assets are not at risk of being seized by creditors.

Liquidity – Money immediately available.

LPP – Swiss law providing for retirement benefits.

M

Macroeconomy – Term in economics relating to global economic data.

Microeconomy – Term in economics relating to individual human behaviour.

Monetarism – Economic theory, founded by Milton Friedman, emphasising monetary policy as the regulator of economic activity.

Monetary base – Money issued by the central bank, comprising cash (banknotes and coins) and bank deposits at the central bank.

Monetary policy – Decisions by the central bank, part of State economic policy.

Money – Legal tender for payment – money can be physical (bank notes and coins) or bank money (bank accounts and electronic money).

Money laundering – Hiding evidence of the irregular or fraudulent origin of a sum of money.

Money supply – Total of money in circulation in the economy, including physical money (bank notes and coins) and bank money (bank accounts and electronic money).

Monopoly – Market in which only one company buys or exploits a given good or service.

Mortgage rate – Interest rate for loans guaranteed by mortgage of real estate.

Multilateral – Relationship between several States, for example in WTO.

N

Neoliberalism – Modern form of liberalism, associated with the theories of Milton Friedman and Friedrich von Hayek.

O

OECD – Organisation for Economic Co-operation and Development, comprising 37 industrialised countries, publisher of many economic studies.

Oil shock – Economic shock caused by a drastic fall in oil supply (the two main shocks were in 1973 and 1979).

Oligopoly – Market in which a small number of companies buy or exploit a given good or service.

Operating account – Table showing all revenue and costs of a company during a given accounting period.

P

Pension fund – Investment fund for financing the employee pensions of one or more companies.

Poverty line – Baseline allowing identification of the sector of population considered poor – varies from country to country.

Primary – Economic sector comprising production of primary materials (agriculture, fisheries, mining, etc.).

Privatisation – Transfer of State enterprises to the private sector.

Productivity – Relationship between a given amount of goods produced and the resources required for their production.

Profit – Revenue less all company costs.

Progressivity – Taxation that increases in proportion to the taxable amount.

Protectionism – Policy preventing foreign companies from competing with national companies.

Public company – Company in which a controlling interest is held by the State or other government entities.

Public debt – All the debt of a public entity, often resulting from cumulative past deficits.

Public service – All State services provided in the general interest of the population.

Purchasing power– Quantity of goods and services that can be acquired with a given sum of money.

R

Recession – Phase of economic stagnation or negative growth.

Recovery – Turning point after a recession prior to a new phase of economic expansion.

S

SDC – Swiss Agency for Development and Co-operation, part of the federal foreign ministry.

SECO – State Secretariat for Economic Affairs – part of the federal department for economics.

Secondary – Economic sector comprising transformation of primary materials into finished industrial products.

Share – Financial instrument representing a part of the capital of a limited company.

SIX Swiss Exchange – Swiss stock market based in Zurich.

SME – Small and medium-sized enterprises (less than 250 employees).

SMI – Swiss Market Index, the main index of the Swiss share market, reflecting the performance of some twenty of the largest Swiss companies.

Speculative bubble – Situation in which the stock market value of companies is overvalued.

Stagnation – Near zero economic growth.

Stock market index – Index of the stock market performance of a given group of companies.

Structural – Linked to the fundamental conditions and structures of the economy.

Subsidy – Financial aid provided to a company by the State in order to promote activity in the general interest.

Supply – Quantity of goods and services available for sale at a given price.

Sustainable development – Concept of development that takes account of present needs without compromising the needs of future generations.

T

Tax – State levy on earnings and property of persons and companies.

Tax haven – Territory with advantageous tax structure.

Technical analysis – A method that uses statistics to analyse market trends.

Tertiary – Economic sector comprising services (administration, trading, banks, etc.).

Trade Union – Group defending workers' interests

Turnover – Total sales of a company in a given accounting period.

W

Working poor – Persons who have work but remain poor.

World Bank – International institution active in development financing.

WTO – World Trade Organisation, body implementing rules for international trade.

Index

Switzerland in a Nutshell

Bergli's In a Nutshell books are entertaining introductions to the key areas of Swiss culture. Illustrated by Mix & Remix, and written by experts in their respective fields, the titles in this series were the winners of the Albert Oeri Democracy Prize.

Swiss Democracy in a Nutshell

96 pages
ISBN 978-3-905252-63-7

Swiss History in a Nutshell

96 pages
ISBN 78-3-905252-19-4

Swissness in a Nutshell

128 pages
ISBN 978-3-905252-65-1

Bergli's bestselling and award-winning Nutshell guides are available at www.bergli.ch and wherever books are sold.